W0050154

Hariprasad Chaurasia

Breath of
Gold

।। श्री हरिप्रसाद चौरसिया को समर्पित शब्द सुमन ।।

सागर-सी गरिमा, शांत-सौम्य
तुम कृष्ण-कला बन छाए हो ।
तुम मधुर-मधुर स्वर, सृष्टि-रुप
अब 'हरि प्रसाद' बन आए हो ।।

पहले 'गोलोक' तुम्हें भाया
'द्वापर' में तुम गोकुलवासी ।
अब पृथ्वी पर मुरली गूंजी
बन बैठे वृंदावन वासी ।।

तुम दिव्य-कला के हो साधक
बांसुरी-वाद्य के आराधक ।
लय-स्वर, गति, तुमसे संचालित
संगीत-विधा के संरक्षक ।।

तुमरे सुर का सुनकर निनाद
यह सारा विश्व अचंभित है ।
सब अपना-आपा भूल रहे
मुरली या फूल सुगंधित है ?

बाँसुरिया छेड़ी है तुमने
या सामवेद की स्वरावली ?
बंसी है या बरसाने की
सुर में डूबी राधिका-लली ?

बाँसुरिया मधुर बजाकर ही
'श्री कृष्ण' ने पाई थी 'राधा' ।
अब 'हरि प्रसाद' इस धरती पर
इसलिए प्राप्त है 'अनुराधा' ।।

A Bouquet in Praise of Shri Hariprasad Chaurasia

Holding the depth of oceans in your calm
You rise above music with your divine art,
Sweet, melodious harmonies, you who embody the universe,
As Hariprasad have taken form.

At first you were enchanted by Golokh
And in Dwapar, you chose to be Gokul-wasi,
Now when the flute sings on earth
You have become Vrindavan-wasi.

Practitioner of your celestial art
Worshipper of the bamboo flute
Rhythm, tune, cadence, are all in your grasp
You guard the knowledge of music in your heart.

As it listens to the sounds you create
The entire world stands in awe
Forgetting themselves each one asks
Is this the scent of flowers, or a flute that plays?

Is it the flute you so sweetly play
Or the tuneful syllables of Sama Ved?
Is it a flute that we see
Or Radhika in musical ecstasy?

Thus through the sweet playing of the flute
Did Sri Krishna win his consort Radha—
Now Hariprasad plays his tunes on earth
And wins for himself, his Anuradha.

ये प्रकृति-पुरूष, धरती औ ' गगन
तुमरी बंसी के सब बंदी ।
लय, ताल, राग-रागिनी सभी
संगीत तुम्हारा संबंधी ।।

नहीं अहंकार, तुम नमित-नमित
संगीत-ध्येय, संगीत लक्ष्य ।
संगीत तुम्हारा ईश्वरीय
संगीत का तुम समझे रहस्य ।।

तुम सरस्वती के हो सुपुत्र
जीवन को जीवन देते हो ।
आलाप-तान लयकारी से
पतझड़-बसंत कर देते हो ।।

गुरू-शिष्य प्रथा दोहराई है
हर शिष्य तुम्हारा मान बने ।
हर शिष्य पायेगा हरि प्रसाद
तुम हृदय-हृदय के प्राण बने ।।

कितना भी लिखूं, लगता अपूर्ण
कम पड़ते हैं ये शब्द-सुमन ।
अनुपम-साधक, स्वर योगी को
'माया गोविंद' का बहुत नमन ।।

—माया गोविंद

Universe, man, earth and sky
Remain captivated by your music
Melody, rhythm, raga and ragini
All music remains linked to your energy.

Not proud, but gentle, humble
Music your aim, melody your goal,
Through music you have found your God
And unravelled its secret stores.

Beloved son of goddess Saraswati,
You give new meaning to our lives
Through alaap, taan, musical virtuosity
You change autumn to spring's bounty.

Inheritor of the guru-shishya tradition
Every student adds to your fame
With Hari's prasad as every student's gain
Their hearts sing praises of your name.

All my writing seems incomplete
My bouquet of words inadequate
To the matchless flautist, the music yogi
Maya Govind dedicates this offering.

—Translated by Sathya Saran

Hariprasad Chaurasia
Breath of *Gold*

~∞~

SATHYA SARAN

EBURY
PRESS

An imprint of Penguin Random House

EBURY PRESS

USA | Canada | UK | Ireland | Australia
New Zealand | India | South Africa | China | Singapore

Ebury Press is part of the Penguin Random House group of companies
whose addresses can be found at global.penguinrandomhouse.com

Published by Penguin Random House India Pvt. Ltd
4th Floor, Capital Tower 1, MG Road,
Gurugram 122 002, Haryana, India

First published in Ebury Press by Penguin Random House India 2019

Copyright © Sathya Saran 2019

All rights reserved

10 9 8 7 6 5 4

This book is a work of non-fiction. The views and opinions expressed herein are
solely those of the author and do not reflect or represent views and opinions held
by any other person. This book is based on the interactions and experiences of
the author and reflects the author's own understanding and conception of such
interactions and experiences.

ISBN 9780670092512

Typeset in Adobe Garamond Pro by Manipal Technologies Limited, Manipal
Printed at Replika Press Pvt. Ltd.

This book is sold subject to the condition that it shall not, by way of trade
or otherwise, be lent, resold, hired out, or otherwise circulated without the
publisher's prior consent in any form of binding or cover other than that in
which it is published and without a similar condition including this condition
being imposed on the subsequent purchaser.

www.penguin.co.in

To all lovers of music,
and especially of the flute

Foreword

Ustad Amjad Ali Khan

In the age of record stores, it was rare to go into a record shop and not see a recording of Pandit Hari Prasad Chaurasia, the master of the bansuri or bamboo flute. One of India's most popular artistes, he is a man on a mission and defies his age to meet his commitments. His zest and passion for sharing his music with music lovers of the world are noteworthy. He is in Mumbai today, Paris tomorrow and San Francisco the day after, with performances on all three days. His endearing persona and ease with people of all ages enhance his popularity. A master of his craft, he is an example to the world of music.

In the year 1960, I met a vibrant Pandit Hariprasad Chaurasia at the Astoria Hotel, Churchgate, with our common friend the virtuoso sitar player Ustad Rais Khan. (If you look at the history of legendary musicians of India, most of them have come up from very humble backgrounds.) Pt Hariprasad Chaurasia is the greatest example of our ancient and historical guru–shishya parampara.

Hari-ji has given a different dimension to the bansuri. The flute is now a universal instrument of the world. When you think of the flute or bansuri, you remember the name of Pt Hariprasad Chaurasia.

In the year 1985, the Haafiz Ali Khan awards were instituted in the name of my father and guru. The award has been given to musicians who have become monumental icons and pioneers of their field in their lifetime. The award ceremonies have taken place in India and in Europe in the past, but now take place at the historic Sarod Ghar: The Museum of Musical Heritage in Gwalior. I was fortunate and honoured to have presented the Haafiz Ali Khan Award to Hari-ji in Gwalior in 1999. Hari-ji and I have participated in many music festivals both in India and overseas from the 1970s onwards.

Undoubtedly, he is very fortunate to have a wife and life partner like Anuradha-ji who herself is a great singer. I remember the milestone series Hari-ji and Angu Bhabhi, as she is fondly referred to, produced, *Sadhana*, based on the lives of musicians of India. This was a TV serial that went on to become the first of its kind.

It is always an evening full of laughter and mutual respect whenever we meet in Hari-ji's residence or at our residence. Hari-ji and my wife Subhalakshmi-ji converse in Bengali. I am also so happy to see the Vrindaban Gurukul institution established by Hari-ji in Mumbai. I had a memorable performance recently at this beautiful establishment in his presence. I would love to visit his Gurukul in Bhubaneswar too in the near future!

The musical message of Pandit Hariprasad Chaurasia will always be carried forward through his able disciples and music lovers. Hari-ji has inspired many young flautists and has given a different meaning to tonal quality; his whole approach is so fresh and unique. Hari-ji is an embodiment of Lord Krishna. I pray for his long healthy musical journey for many years ahead.

Prelude

Ustad Zakir Hussain

In India it is believed that a son of a great and legendary artist will also be a great artist. By that account, Pt Hariprasad Chaurasia should have been a wrestler. Everything was as it should be at his birth—his father was a wrestler and his new born son would now be able to carry on the tradition. BUT NO! The spirits had other ideas. It was not by chance that the boy was named Hariprasad. There was great manipulation in progress and the spirits had ordained a different path with a very bright future for this baby. Lord Krishna himself decided to once again live amongst mere humans, thus the eleventh avatar. Bhagwan Krishna himself breathed the powerful swaras of his bansi into the baby's lungs and bid him to go forth and spread happiness amongst the listeners.

Hari-ji, as the world fondly addresses him, is a very simple human being, not threatened by the lure of maya, but his music is as complex, deep and meaningful as the shlokas of the Bhagavadgita. Lord Krishna has moulded Hari-ji's music in his image and the whole world rejoices in this wondrous revelation.

I consider Hari-ji one of my mentors. With his and the great Shivkumar Sharma-ji's guidance, I was able to decipher and arrive at the understanding of how my tabla playing should be. I cannot thank Hari-ji enough for what he has given me. He is undoubtedly the greatest Bansuri Vidwan of our time and for many centuries to come. We are fortunate to have seen and heard him perform, and I pray that may these powerful swaras keep regaling us for many more decades.

This book is special because it provides the reader an inside glimpse of Hari-ji, his music and his life. I am glad that we, the fans, admirers and worshippers of this genius spirit, have a chance to know him better through this book. A very good read indeed.

Introduction

Birju Maharaj was reliving moments from his journey as a dancer. He spoke with gusto, and often broke into song, his voice clear and in perfect tune.

We were at a gathering at the Vrindaban Gurukul in Mumbai, guests of Pt Hariprasad Chaurasia and his family, invited to listen to the Kathak maestro. As the evening progressed and we listened and watched enraptured, I looked around to check where Pandit-ji was sitting. It had been a long time since we had met.

He looks frail, I told myself, very different from what I remembered of him, a man of quick strides and easy laughter. He sat listening to his friend as the stories unravelled, a quiet, unobtrusive part of the audience. Looking at him no one would guess his stature as a legendary performer who has created musical history with an instrument as humble as the flute.

It struck me then that the world needed to know more about Pt Hariprasad Chaurasia. His journey, his achievements, his struggles . . . there had to be a story behind that quiet presence, one that could inspire and elevate readers. And which needed to be chronicled for future generations.

At the first opportunity, I messaged Pandit-ji's son, Rajeev, whose number had been on the RSVP. Why not do a book on

Pandit-ji? I could facilitate it. 'Just what I was thinking,' came the response on my phone.

I went back with a few tentative names of possible writer–musicians. But was told that the decision had been taken. That I would be the person to write the book. I learnt later that I had Pandit-ji's old friend, S.D. Burman, to thank for this. Rajeev and his wife, Pushpanjali, had read my biography of the composer. Could I shape this biography in a similar way? Hari-ji's instant approval of me as the biographer, which followed soon after, added just the right impetus. I plunged into researching the book. I was happy it would give me a chance to know the maestro better.

Strangely enough, our paths had been crossing unexpectedly through the years. I had been recruited to write a couple of scripts for *Sadhana*, a serial on musical greats produced by Hari-ji's wife, Anuradha Chaurasia. Sometime later, I had been contacted by HMV to write the sleeve notes for the Shiv–Hari LP *The Valley Recalls*, that followed their wonderful first collaboration, *Call of the Valley*. I am not sure if the write-up was used, but it was a fun assignment.

But the most memorable of all was when I was called to the phone one day at work. The voice at the other end introduced itself as Hariprasad Chaurasia. And asked if I would like to go with a team of musicians to Oslo, to listen to them performing. And that was my first real encounter with Hari-ji.

Over the three days of watching Hari-ji, Zakir Hussain and Viku Vinayakram interact with one another, and listening to their music, I learnt a lot about the camaraderie that exists among musicians who are confident of their art, and unparalleled in their chosen fields. There was no one-upmanship, no flaunting of artistic airs. Instead, much jollity and conversation. And of course, great music.

I discovered more when I started researching this book. Perhaps nothing symbolizes Hari-ji's personality as perfectly as the instrument he loves. Like the flute, he is simple, with no trappings; close to nature, unchanged by artifice. Like the flute, his quiet humility belies the power that his music holds . . . the power to move, to create emotion, to build a rapport with all who listen to him play. And like the flute, I have found its player, too, is in his own way, beloved of the gods.

Over a year of sporadic interactions, I have learnt much more. He never gives up, and nothing can keep him from his music. Not the trembling of his hand, not a sudden shortness of breath. He overcomes it all with the strength of his will and his ability to laugh off every hurdle age places in his path. Under his sage-like demeanour is a crackling sense of humour and a rapier-sharp wit. Anyone who knows him well knows how quick his repartees can be, balanced by a gentleness of nature that ensures the humour is most often turned against himself, and never aimed at others.

But it was in how others look at him that my biggest discovery about Hari-ji lay. The mere mention of his name to anyone who asked what my next book was about would evoke a softening of the eyes, and an indulgent smile. It made me think that irrespective of age and station, most people regarded Hariprasad Chaurasia not just as a flautist of great merit. Instead, they saw in his childlike simplicity of heart and his love for his flute the qualities of yet another flute player who charmed all who heard him and cast a spell on them with his music. Hari-ji's flute seemed to have the power to take anyone into the realm of myth, letting them roam the grassy meadows of Vrindavan, lost in its melody.

Little wonder, students from all over the world gather under his shade. Young and old, Indian and foreign. And while some come leaving jobs and family to nestle in his gurukuls, others who must work, find ways to make time to learn.

Let me share a story. My friend Sumant Batra had just landed in Mumbai and was taking an Uber to the hotel where he had all-day meetings, including with me. When he noticed that the driver had a flute on the passenger seat beside him, he asked the man if he played the instrument. According to Batra, the driver not only said he did play the flute, but driving the car to the side of the road, parked it, and played a tune. When Batra complimented him on his playing, he responded proudly that he was a student of Pt Hariprasad Chaurasia.

Like most great gurus, Hariprasad Chaurasia packages music with lessons on the art of simple and meaningful living that enriches the soul of his students. In fact, researching this book has enriched me in many ways. As I gathered the snatches of music, the stories from his life, and the words from his interviews to weave them into this book, I realized the tapestry of my own thought and understanding had acquired richer colours. I hope the story between these pages will do the same for every reader. In fact, I am sure it will.

Sathya Saran

Bombay, Main Lawns, CCI

13 December 2018

At last the evening was upon him. It was his turn. Why did he feel such heaviness in his heart?

Everything had gone perfectly. Young Kaushiki had sung with feeling. Amjad Ali Khan, Birju Maharaj, Shivkumar Sharma, Zakir Hussain, Nityanand Haldipur, all of them had gathered without hesitation to pay homage. Each unparalleled in his field, each had held his own. Flute and voice, sarod and ghungroo, santoor and song, the notes had risen like offerings to circle around the portrait of his guruma. He looked at the picture of Annapurna Devi undulating gently on the backdrop and closed his eyes. He remembered her smile, rare, but like sunlight breaking through monsoon clouds. In this photograph, though, she looked teary-eyed, as if despairing of the state of the world. But they had found a likeness in no other image that allowed enlarging.

Far away, the audience was clapping. He stepped on to the stage. It was his turn to offer shraddhanjali to his guruma.

He smiled at Shivkumar who was already seated in place. Trusted friend, companion in music through the years. Together they had made history. Regaled audiences. But today, they would offer respect. Humble. Sincere. Today, they would play for Guruma.

His heart swelled at the first cadence of the santoor.

The audience took a deep breath. Here were well-loved sounds, the blending of flute and santoor, one lifting the soul to float high in the skies, the other carrying the listener through babbling brooks and flower-filled fields.

He picked up the flute. Placed it to his lips. Just so. A gesture as familiar as taking breath. He inhaled deep, till his lungs were full. They had held him in good stead, belying the passing of years. He could hold his own on the flute, hour after hour, never flagging, letting his breath transform into music, enchanting and unique. Pursing his lips, he played the first note.

His heart fluttered. The note was flat. I am tired, he thought. Heavy with distress. But I must play. He blew into the flute. Flat again. And yet again. Where was the resonance? And the effortless lift?

The audience waited, hushed. The stars held their breath. Such a thing had never happened to him before, and yet, today, his flute would not sing! His breath . . . the santoor sang out, camouflaging the chaos clanging in his mind. Bless you, Shiv-ji, he thought, as he prepared to try once more.

By the end of the evening, he had barely played a few notes. The heaviness in his heart muffled the applause.

Why, he asked, of the eyes that looked back at him from the portrait. *You who were mother, teacher, guru, all in one, why did you abandon me? Was I such a poor pupil that you could not accept my offering?*

The next day, they rushed him to the hospital where the doctor inserted three stents into his heart.

He smiled when he came out of the operation theatre. *It was not you*, he intoned to his guruma. *It was my stupid heart. Acting its age! I will play yet again*, he whispered a promise.

Allahabad

(1938–1957)

Hariprasad had always been a good pupil. Even if an unwilling one.

'Unwilling' was indeed putting it mildly. He hated it all. Waking up as the cock crowed in the distance, rubbing oil on the body even as the sun was still a sleepy red blob on the horizon. No soft sari pallu to wipe his face after he had washed it . . . Instead, a strong-armed father waiting at the akhada. He hated the routine, the daily exercises, the fact that every bout in the mud ended up with an opponent sitting on him, pinning him to the ground, and keeping him there endlessly. His bones ached at night. But he was a good pupil. An obedient son. When your father is Chedilal Pehelwan, often referred to reverentially simply as 'Pehelwan sahib', a renowned wrestler who believed that the best way to bring up motherless children was to teach them to wrestle, it was safer being obedient.

Pehelwan sahib might have struck fear in many a heart, but he was a good albeit strict father. Choosing not to marry again after his wife's death, he took upon himself the upbringing of his three surviving children—Hariprasad, his elder sister and his younger brother. Hariprasad remembers the freshly ground almonds, and from the thronging street shops of Allahabad, the delicious, rich, ghee-soaked jalebis, rabdi and milk rich with cream as part of his dietary regimen.

He remembers too that music fascinated him from the earliest years of his life. 'When I was a baby, my mother would sing lullabies to me. She wanted me to sleep very well. And she would sing. And I would listen properly. Perhaps my love of music started then.'

Both his father and his uncle sang bhajans, and the boy also found himself responding to the music that filled the temple courtyard in the early evenings. Memory often mingles with legend when one delves into the origins of iconic talent, and the story goes that one day, the priest, who often saw the young Hariprasad singing bhajans with the others, asked him to sing solo.

The boy, unabashed, sat down and let his voice flow. When the pandit mentioned it to Pehelwan sahib the next day, elaborating that his son was musically blessed and could carry a song wonderfully well, the father was only slightly impressed. Music was for the rich, an indulgence that the likes of his family could not afford. If the boy chose to sing at the temple, that was fine, but his real future lay in the akhada. He still had a long way to go, but he would learn.

And indeed, the hours in the mud pit were helping in ways yet inscrutable. The easiest way to wash off the grime and mud was to jump into the river, where the strong currents would cleanse, soothe and cool the body. The river also held a promise of forbidden fruit . . . luscious, ripe melons and cucumbers grew on the other bank, and it was not long before, his body strengthened by the hours of exercise, Hariprasad could keep pace with the older boys and swim right across the river to steal and gorge on all they could plunder.

Other temptations beckoned as well. A new neighbour had shifted in. In close-knit communities, such comings and goings usually draw many curious onlookers, and chances are Hariprasad too watched as the man and his wife moved with their belongings into the house that stood next to his own, divided only by a common wall.

His curiosity was piqued when he heard music floating out from within. He saw young people about his own age, coming and going. It dawned on him that the man who occupied the house was a singer who taught music. Hariprasad even knew some of the bhajans he was teaching. How wonderful if he could learn too! It would invoke the unique feeling of peace that he often felt as he sang at the temple.

He hit upon a ruse. Singing rather loudly, he wandered about, close to the house. Often, the singer's wife, looking for a subject on which to lavish her thwarted maternal affections, would invite him to taste something she had cooked. Hariprasad would gladly partake of the delights offered. And at every opportunity, he would sing, hoping the teacher would listen and be impressed.

A singer's ears are ever alert to music, and it was not long before Raja Ram, as the neighbour was called, heard the youngster singing and called out to him.

Raja Ram was a kindly man, a dhrupad singer who earned by teaching bhajans. Childless, he and his wife enjoyed listening to the young voices resounding in their home for the brief duration of the classes. The music eased away the shadow of loneliness that looms over couples who face old age without their offspring around them to brighten their path.

When Hariprasad, elated that his ruse had worked, sat cross-legged and earnest in front of his future teacher and sang a film song, Raja Ram was overjoyed. He realized the boy had a natural gift for music; though untaught, he could carry a tune.

Master and pupil delighted in each other. Soon, the lessons, surreptitious and unknown to Pehelwan sahib, were well under way. Realizing that Hariprasad could push beyond the calibre of most of his other students, Raja Ram started teaching him the rules of classical singing, step by step. The young student bounded up the steps admirably, with enthusiasm.

Hindustani classical music demands of its singers a substantial range of voice. Being able to sing in an octave higher as well as lower than one's normal pitch ensures the singer can glide up and down with ease as he delineates a raga decorated with intricate taans.

To his disappointment, Raja Ram soon discovered that his ardent pupil was limited in range. His voice would never rise beyond the low octave. But seeing that the boy was indeed devoted to learning music, and that his lungs had the power to hold a note steady for a long time, Raja Ram suggested Hariprasad find an instrument that made use of his breath, and continue his journey.

'I could not afford an instrument like the sitar, which was very popular at that time,' Hariprasad recounted in an interview organized by the NCPA. 'The flute was easily available, it was sold at festivals and fairs. It was cheap. Besides, I had seen it with Lord Krishna. It was always a part of him in the temples, whether he was alone or with Radha, and I knew it was one of the oldest instruments. It was so simple too, no strings to tune, no leather to maintain. Just a stick of bamboo with holes, and one had only to blow into it to create sound. I chose the flute.'

Now he lacked a teacher. Not surprisingly, he found he could get the flute to respond to his breath. The sounds were sweet and almost musical, as he knew the scales and could try and work on playing them on his newfound instrument. Like many other musically inclined greats who floundered before finding their guru, the young musician turned to the radio for guidance.

'I would listen very carefully,' he remembers. 'Be it a singer or an instrumentalist, I would try to grasp the flow of the melody, the way they worked the notes. I am a learner still, I continue my learning. And over the years, I have learnt so much by listening to the greats . . . Ustad Allauddin Khan, whom I met, my Guruma Annapurna Devi, Ravi Shankar-ji, Ustad Ali Akbar Khan sahab, Ustad Vilayat Khan sahab, Ustad Amir Khan sahab . . . but as a boy of nine or ten, the music from the radio was my primary teacher. When the flute played over the radio, I would listen very carefully. I had a *lagaav* with the sound; I wanted to play at least 1 per cent of the sound . . .'

It was the radio that led him to his next guru. When a mesmerizing flute recital ended, he listened attentively to catch the name of the performer. Bholanath Prasanna. Determined to find him, Hariprasad rented a bike and rode to the radio station, and met Bholanath. 'He had four or five hours' duty, so he took me to the canteen. Once he was free, he took me to his modest house just behind the radio station. "You can meet me here," he told me.'

Hariprasad remembers it all very clearly. 'The place was called Draupadi Bagh, named after the river Draupadi. I parked my rented bike and knocked on his door, which was quickly opened.' He did not know it then, but the nine-year-old had just opened the door to his future.

Bholanath was one of three brothers, each of whom was adept at playing more than one instrument. Between them they could play the flute, shehnai and sarod, all very melodiously, and the younger brother, Raghunath Prasanna played the shehnai at weddings.

Bholanath lived alone when his brothers were not visiting from their hometown, Varanasi. He would gather two or three young students around and teach them. It was a simple gurukul kind of relationship between teacher and disciple. On holidays, after a morning lesson, the boys would cut vegetables or grind masala; Bholanath would then cook a meal for all of them, and send them home after lunch. Sometimes, there would be lessons in swimming at the Draupadi Ghat.

'He would make simple flutes for us,' Hariprasad remembers. 'He would choose bamboo pieces that he ascertained were free of insects, season the lengths of bamboo in oil, and then fashion them into flutes for each of us. It was such a thrill!'

Once his duty at the radio station was done, Bholanath would spend all his time with the children, often adding outings on bikes to eat jalebis or to watch the *Ram Lila*. If his father wondered where the boy was through the long hours after school, the young student had his answer ready—he was of course at the library, studying.

According to Hariprasad, the unstructured teaching method nurtured the feeling that music was not just a learning, but something to be shared as a source of joy. It was sacred too, worthy of worship. 'I found my yoga in the flute. Even today, my atma speaks through the flute,' he says.

'Actually, I did not have to study very hard,' Hariprasad continues, referring to his school days. 'In school, they would ask me to play the flute for a few minutes whenever a VIP would visit. It made me the teachers' favourite because I was always ready to oblige. Naturally, I never failed in the exams; they would add a few marks and make me pass, if I fell short.'

Impressed by his ability to play the flute at such a young age, teachers would bless the boy. 'Try to become like Tansen,' they would say, but Hariprasad insists he had no such ambitions. 'I was happy getting into mischief with friends, playing film songs on the flute, and of course, I was still going to the akhada to keep my father happy. He was quite pleased too, as he believed I was following in his footsteps.'

Pandit Hariprasad Chaurasia often recounts with delight a story from the days of his early adventures with the flute. Of how, one hot afternoon, he found himself captivated when he heard another young boy playing a tune on his flute. He followed the sound, much like a child following the Pied Piper. What was in that instrument that created such a melodious sound, he wondered.

Within minutes, he got a chance to unravel the mystery. The player had reached a tap, and placing the flute on the ground, had cupped his hands to drink his fill of water. Quick as a magpie, Hariprasad swooped down, picked up the flute and started to run away.

'Of course the boy gave chase,' he says, recalling the episode. 'But I was fast and strong and knew my way around, so I escaped being caught by turning into a narrow lane between houses. The flute was mine. Actually, there is nothing to be read into the story. The episode did not change my life or affect my musical journey in any way. It was just a bit of boyish mischief.'

His prowess with the flute helped him land assignments on the radio for children's programmes, almost once a month. The short film piece or tune he would play would earn a handsome five rupees, his first earnings ever.

An Interlude

Two runaways on a train hurtling its way to Bombay. The boys sit shoulder to shoulder, crammed into a third-class compartment. The rat-a-tat of the wheels on the wooden sleepers is comforting enough to lull them into a drowsy state, but hunger keeps them awake. Hunger, and fear. For our stowaways are travelling without tickets.

Thus, one sleeps while the other keeps a wary watch for the man in uniform, the ticket checker. At the first sight of him, they run into the bathroom, bravely bearing the stink and the filth until they believe it is safe to come out again. Once they reach Bombay, everything will fall into place, they say to each other for comfort.

But the city thwarts them. They have come searching for stardom, the flautist and his friend, Jagannath, who is a singer. For two days, they walk around trying to enter studios where films are shot. At night, they seek shelter in a temple, and lead the bhajan-singing in order to get a meal in return.

On the third day, they give up, and find a train to take them back. The return journey is again edged with fear, laced with the stench of the toilet they frequently find themselves having to hide in. Bereft of the hope that had kept them buoyant on their way in, the boys are a sad, disheartened lot.

The only silver lining to the story is that, overjoyed at his son coming back, the distraught father is so relieved, he forgets to give him a thrashing.

Some meetings are fated; destiny ensures they happen. Hariprasad was still very young when the meeting that would completely change his life and career took place. He was playing with his friend at Kailash Hotel, which the other boy's father owned. 'It was near the station,' Hariprasad explains.

'Every month, Baba Allauddin Khan of Maihar would come to Allahabad to play at the radio station, which was behind the railway station. Allahabad was a huge centre for music, almost every big artiste came there for the festivals held annually. But Baba came every month and would stay at Kailash Hotel.

'I did not know it then, but Baba was an amazing man. He was the first to play dhrupad in instruments; no one else was doing it. He played the trumpet in classical mode, played the piano, the ghatam, which is just an upturned clay pot, he would whistle classical music in the dhrupad style . . . I have never seen such a personality anywhere else.

'Anyway, we boys were sitting outside, and we could hear Baba in his room, practising, and [we could] smell his bidi.

'Baba came out to ask what we were doing. "Come sing with me," he said. I told him I do not sing, I play the flute. So he asked me to get my flute. When I went the next day, he sat me down beside him, and started to play his violin. "Play your flute with me," he said. I started to accompany him.

'We played together for a while, then stopped. "The scales are different, but you kept the tune," he said. And he smiled.'

Allauddin Khan was a strict teacher, but he had a very kind face. His eyes crinkled at the corners and his cheeks became like apples when he smiled. 'Come with me to Maihar, I will teach you,' he told Hariprasad.

The boy demurred. 'My father is a pehelwan, he will kill me if he learns of my desire,' he said. 'He does not like me to learn music.'

Khan sahab sighed. Perhaps he knew he had lost the chance to help yet another star shine bright. The young lad could have joined his pantheon of students that included his son-in-law Ravi Shankar, his daughter Annapurna, his son Ali Akbar Khan, Pannalal Ghosh and many others.

'In case you desire to come later, and I am too old, go to my daughter, Annapurna, in Bombay,' he said, placing a hand on the boy's head.

The meeting made a deep impression on Hariprasad. He would hold the advice close to his heart, and open his secret package of hope many years later, standing at the crossroads of his life.

An Interlude

Dressed in shorts and shirt, hair slicked back, the young flautist stands in the wings. A crowd is gathering at Prabhat Talkies, where Manik Verma, a well-known singer, is slated to perform. Hariprasad has been asked to play a short, fifteen-minute piece before the main artiste takes the stage. It is the organizer's way of keeping the audience from getting restive while the hall fills slowly.

Nervous though he is, Hariprasad takes a deep breath, wipes his sweaty palms on the sides of his shorts, and at a signal from the opposite side of the wings, steps on to the stage to face the mike.

Once the flute touches his lips, the boy is transformed. He is lost in his music, and though many in the audience, somewhat surprised, quieten down to listen, he is blissfully unaware of their existence. Then, he is done. His eyes darting to take a quick look at the crowd in front of him, he runs to the wings and doesn't stop until he is out of the venue. His heart is beating fast again, once the spell of the flute is broken. He rushes to the bus stop. He does not know it, but the audience is asking Manik Verma why they could not hear more of the young flute player. It was possibly the first of the many requests for encores he would receive in his career as a musician.

His constant companion now, the flute never leaves his hands. All day it stays by his side; at night, it nestles, hidden by his pillow.

His dilemma is a constant one. Where can he find a place to practise—quiet, undisturbed? Where his father would not find him. He seeks out the riverside. There, sitting by the flowing water, under a tree, he finds the peace he seeks, as he lifts the flute to his lips. Other times, he walks to find empty stretches of land, where he can sit by himself. The hours pass as he plays, engrossed, and it is only when the sun paints his surroundings in changed colours that he realizes how long he has been gone.

Reluctantly, at such times, he rises and walks back slowly, thoughtfully. In his mind, the tune he has been delineating continues to play incessantly.

Those born into the lap of musical families have a readymade path that lies ahead of them, where the seeds of their talent can bloom. Fathers or uncles take on their tutelage right from the start, and through lessons in listening and practice, lead them towards finding their own space among the luminaries of the gharana. Then, it is up to each one to unfold the enigma of style, content and presentation that will build on what the elders in the gharana had to offer, and thereon to find their place in the sun.

Those born into non-musical families, or families that did not consider music a profession worth pursuing, have to swim upstream for a long time before finding the freedom to follow their dream.

If Mukesh, the famed yesteryear playback singer, had to abandon dreams of singing and studies after Class Ten and get a job with the Delhi Department of Public Works to support his family income, and if K.L. Saigal had to sell typewriters to get by, Hariprasad did not fare any better. School finals over, a very average marksheet under his belt, and definitely wishing to avoid further thrashings in the akhada, the young man sought employment as a means of escape.

His search resulted in his landing the job of a lower division clerk at the Allahabad Milling Company.

'Everyone knew me because of my flute. So, though I was underage for employment, I was taken on.' Hariprasad remembers Kanoria, who owned the company, as a kind soul. 'He knew I was motherless, and instructed his office to feed me. There was a lot of love in his heart for me. I was about sixteen, and was quite overwhelmed.'

The job also gave him the opportunity to continue his lessons. Hariprasad would run off to Pt Bholanath's place every evening, or whenever the workload was low. To questions from his father, the stock response would be that he had been given an extra load of work.

Short of turning eighteen, with an eye to bettering his prospects, Hariprasad put himself through the tedium of a typing course. It got him a government job.

'To say my father was delighted is saying it mildly,' he remembers. 'He distributed laddoos all over the locality saying, "My son has a government job!"'

But even as he took dictation and typed out letters and reports for the government organization that had hired him, Hariprasad continued his lessons. His two constant gurus now were the radio and Pt Bholanath.

Occasionally, the city would also throw up opportunities for first-hand learning. Allahabad's annual music and culture fests would attract the greats of the time, who would take to the stage in the late evening and perform one after the other, through the night. Bleary-eyed with sleep, his ears resounding with the music and rhythms he had heard, Hariprasad, who would have crept out under cover of darkness once his father started snoring, would sneak back home before the sun rose, and crawl into bed, before his father woke at 5 a.m. to start his morning rituals.

Not surprisingly, there were many in Allahabad who cast an indulgent eye upon the young man who would never be seen without his flute. In his book *Woodwinds of Change*, Surjit Singh lists the supporters who not only encouraged the young flautist, but also helped further his musical education in diverse ways. Among them was Bishambarnath Yadav, a vocalist and violinist adept at playing the harmonium and flute as well. A sweetmeat shop owner, he was a generous soul who gave freely both the goodies in his shop as well as musical advice to the young customer. The latter in turn enjoyed the visits for the double benefit of pandering to his sweet tooth and learning classical compositions from the older man.

Hariprasad's constant search for secret and quiet places to practise his flute ended when Guruprasad Sharma, a violinist, offered him his place for riyaz. In fact, the two would spend hours together practising, discussing music, and often, other musicians would join in.

Surjit Singh also mentions Kailash Nath Vaidya, a *nadi-vaid* whose four children were all musically talented. They would join forces with Hariprasad in performing, his flute getting the support of tabla, harmonium, sitar as well as a vocalist.

At such times, Hariprasad felt his life was complete.

Quite amazingly, despite his regular visits to the radio station to play for children's programmes, Hariprasad's growing reputation as a flautist of exceptional talent escaped Pehelwan sahib's notice.

'I was lucky my father never heard any of it,' Hariprasad jokes. 'If he hit me, who would volunteer to save me!'

Perhaps in these days of hyperactive social media, where achievements are flaunted and milestones celebrated, where video clips reach across the world within seconds, thanks to the Web, it would have been impossible to hide the fact that not only was Hariprasad almost regularly featuring in children's programmes over the radio, but had also been recruited to play as an accompanist in folk music to a dance recital, and had done so at no less an august venue than the Rashtrapati Bhavan itself with President Dr Rajendra Prasad in the audience! Of course, the music-hungry fifteen-year-old must have eagerly absorbed everything he heard when performers of the ilk of the Dagar brothers and Ustad Hafiz Ali Khan sang the same evening.

As an eighteen-year-old now, typing out government memos and letters, Hariprasad continued his visits to the radio station. The sound of instruments being tuned that wafted through half-open doors while artistes waited to enter the sound-proof studios gladdened his heart, and made him feel he was in his element. He was familiar by now with many of the officials at the station, and they in turn looked upon him with kind indulgence. Often, he would unburden his heart to one or the other, expressing his need to concentrate on music above the mundanities that kept him otherwise occupied. Those listening would nod in empathy; the musicians among them could possibly understand his angst.

Surjit Singh writes of Hariprasad giving his audition. The incident bears retelling here.

Picture this: Hariprasad takes his place facing the examiner. There are no sound recorders in the room, no spools of tape waiting to start turning as the audition begins. Technology had yet to catch up with music, which was still best tested by a discerning ear.

The examiner allotted to test the young performer's prowess was a giant in his own right. Prof. Ratanjhankar was renowned as a musician and counted V.G. Jog, a violinist who would go on to be awarded the Padma Bhushan, among his students. Any other examinee might have trembled knowing who was testing him, but Hariprasad says he was quite unaware of just how much an audition could mean for a performer. Besides, he was quite confident of his own abilities.

He played a simple song in Raga Sarang, as was suitable for the time of the day; the audition was in the afternoon. The professor listened gravely and nodded, deciding the instrumentalist should be given a B grade.

Auditions have always remained inscrutable yardsticks. Jagjit Singh, despite being classically trained and adept in the dhrupad style, was classified as a light music artiste. A happy coincidence as hindsight shows, for it channelled his talent, developing him into a trailblazing ghazal singer. Perhaps vidhwans, when they sit in judgement, tend to forget their own learning journey, and judge more strictly than is required.

When Bholanath learnt, after questioning his student about the audition, that he had passed, but with a B grade, he must have felt some disappointment, knowing his pupil's measure of talent. But there was joy in knowing that Hariprasad would be able to maintain his link with the radio. Which was, at that time, the only medium through which an artiste could make himself heard far beyond the parameters of his own surroundings.

Cuttack

(1957–1961)

1957. He watches the terrain swiftly sweep past, as the train rattles along. He is leaving behind everything familiar. Home, family, friends, and those he has shared music with. He wonders what is in store ahead; there is a knot of uncertainty in his mind.

He has never travelled alone, except for that furtive, ill-fated journey with Jagannath to Bombay. But this time he has a ticket in his pocket, a window to lean against, the cool evening wind in his face, and even the luxury of a berth to climb on to at night. All courtesy his new job with All India Radio, popularly known as AIR.

He feels a sudden elation. The akhada will claim him no more. He is a musician, officially. He grips his flute tighter, his talisman, his companion. He now owns more than one instrument, and he smiles when he thinks of the flutes clacking companionably against each other in his suitcase.

His father had come into the room while he was packing them away.

'So many flutes!' he had exclaimed. 'When did you learn to play music?'

'I had told him just a while ago, on the day I was leaving,' Hariprasad remembers, 'and for the first time in my life, I saw my father cry. His eyes filled as he said, "I have tried to be a father and a mother to you children. I did not marry again for your sake, and now you are leaving me alone! If you were so fond of music, you should have told me." I told him I had not dared, I had been afraid of his anger. Now, of course, it was too late.'

His father had been mollified when he told him he was leaving to take up a job at the Cuttack radio station of AIR on a salary of 180 rupees. In those days, that was a sum sure to impress any father, and a clear jump from what the government job had offered. Besides, uncertain as he himself was of whether he would be able to handle life alone in a strange city, Hariprasad told his father he would give it a try for a month, and if things did not work out, he would return.

Certain that the boy would not last long in an unfamiliar place or do anything remarkable enough to be retained at the job, Pehelwan sahib gave him permission to go.

Taking a deep breath, Hariprasad relives the feeling of freedom he got when his father uttered the word 'Go'. He is flying freer than any bird in flight!

The mood lingers as he reaches Calcutta, with its bustling platforms and thronging crowds. Strange calls reach his ears as hawkers walk past, calling out their wares. He has hours to kill before the connecting train that will take him to his destination, so he walks about, taking in the sight of the Howrah Bridge, tasting the clay as he drinks tea from earthen cups, awaiting the Jagannath Puri Express. When it steams in late in the evening, our young flautist boards it and soon falls into a sound, dreamless sleep. But something tells him he will meet his destiny where he is going.

Destiny stood before him in the form of a tall man with a strangely piercing gaze and a kindly smile. As station director, AIR, Cuttack, P.V. Krishnamurthy conducted a short face-to-face with the young man who sat in front of his desk. One quick glance at the wet blotches from the rain still visible on his new staffer's shirt told him that he must have come through early in the morning, for the Jagannath Puri Express disgorges its load of passengers at 5 a.m. every day. And though the young man was looking at him wide-eyed, his face bore the smudge of insufficient sleep. If the older man felt like smiling at the inappropriate shorts and bush shirt that was still Hariprasad's chosen mode of attire, he also felt a tinge of something akin to fatherly concern. The youth was probably travelling this far for the first time, he told himself.

A quick round of questions told him all his assumptions were right.

It was no surprise that the station director took the young staffer under his wing. Hariprasad's obvious naïveté evoked a protective instinct. Maybe the older gentleman sensed it too, that under his simplicity, there blazed a fierce dedication to music, waiting to be fanned aflame.

And so, here he is, AIR's newest staff member. Still at sea, wondering what his role here was going to be. He has planned to live well within his means and send most of his earnings home to his father. Someone told him that he could get a bed in a dormitory for five rupees a month.

But Krishnamurthy has bent the rules a wee bit and told him to occupy the spare room at the station where instruments and other extras are stored.

The room suits Hariprasad just fine. Not only is it bright with the morning light streaming in through the windows, but there is a terrace too, and he can spend evenings there, taking in the green surroundings. Of course, storerooms do not have attached bathrooms. He has been warned that he must not let anyone know he is a stowaway at the premises of the radio station, so he hurries every morning down the stairs, to wash and be ready before the artistes and staffers of the morning shift arrive. Radio stations have morning broadcasts and work starts early in the day. Luckily for him, waking up at the crack of dawn is no problem. The akhada had trained him well in that aspect.

Surprisingly, for a well-staffed radio station in a culturally rich town like Cuttack, Hariprasad is the only flautist on the rolls. The other instrumentalists include violinists, surbahar and sitar players, as well as exponents of the tabla and the sarangi.

It is not very long before Hariprasad makes new friends at his workplace. His ready smile and the unmistakable twinkle in his eyes that hints at a quick sense of humour make him likeable enough. More important is the fact that he brings to their music the added dimension of his flute's melodious accompaniment.

'He was very jovial, very likeable, and cooperative. And we could all see how kind-hearted he was.' Pranab Patnaik, a singer who was a vocalist with AIR Cuttack when Hariprasad was a newcomer there, remembers in detail much of his impressions. 'He had a very different way of playing too. There was a conch-like quality to the sound he produced with the flute. I was with AIR since 1948, he was a regular with me. I respected him for his talent and dedication. Whenever he used to compose, in Studio One, I would be around, listening. In the evenings, we would have coffee. He would tell me, "I have created a *sur*," and I would say, "*Bajaiye, main gaa loonga.*" He would play the flute, I would pick up the tune and sing; that was the understanding.'

Today, Pranab Patnaik lives in Bhubaneswar with his family. At the time of this unscheduled interview, he was recovering from a fever; in fact, he was still running a temperature above 100 degrees when he insisted, 'If you wish to talk about Hari-ji, I will make time.' And though his voice rasps due to the fever, he talks at length, going on to mention the two songs that he sang for a special programme on ghazals on the radio station.

'The programme was titled *Saja Phulo*, meaning fresh flowers. The songs were in Oriya of course, a language that Hariprasad had picked up quite easily. He tuned the songs wonderfully. His method was to depend on the artist, the weight of his voice, range, pitch. He brought out the best of the singer's capabilities. The songs '*Panav potararo tiki nao ka*' and '*Dura nil nava sasil*' are still playing! I sang both. He made tunes for all the main artistes in AIR. We were three of us, and he made songs for each of us. He tuned around sixteen or seventeen songs for me to sing, all in Oriya.

'He's not a flautist, he is a magician; he would attend all classical concerts around Cuttack, anywhere in Orissa, he had his ragas at his fingertips . . . Hari-ji was attached to the National Music Association School during 1955–1960, where I also taught. His students are still there.

'He still remains a dear friend, and our paths crossed many times after he left Cuttack. He never forgets his days in Cuttack,' Patnaik adds.

Patnaik fondly relives the memories. A black-and-white photograph of him from that time looks down upon us, creating a surreal moment. And as the mood takes him, he sings a stanza from one of the two songs he has mentioned.

The tune is sweet and simple. Despite his fever and sore throat, his voice is rich, reminiscent of the tenor of Talat Mahmood's voice. His wife comes running in.

'Don't sing!' she admonishes him. 'Your fever will go up.' Her husband smiles at her and continues, as if to say, you cannot separate a singer from his song. 'At least do not sing the high notes in the antara,' she pleads, but he goes on, voice rising effortlessly, bypassing the irritation that made itself evident in her tone.

When he stops, his cheeks are red, and everyone in the room is moved. Such is the power of music!

Once again, as if leading him by the hand, Hariprasad's destiny would find him a new mentor in music, in the form of Bhubaneswar Mishra.[1]

Perhaps, he saw in Hariprasad a mirror of his own passion for music. Mishra played mentor to the newcomer who was nine years his junior, leading him deeper into the intricacies of classical music. Neither of the two knew it then, but it would be an association that would benefit both musicians and go down in the annals of musical history.

Hariprasad's early days at his new job are now chalked out for him. He is to prepare the artistes who come to the studio, so there is no hitch in the recording or their recitals.

His mind still hungers for knowledge, so he takes up his duties eagerly, and makes the most of every chance he gets to listen to others; absorbing, learning, integrating it all into his consciousness.

---

[1] Widely regarded as the 'Mother of Odissi classical music', Pt Mishra was trained in both Carnatic and Hindustani styles of classical music and was considered a virtuoso on the violin. (Seventeenth death anniversary of Pt Bhubaneswar Mishra; Ratikant Mohapatra, Bhubaneswar. Email: srjan.bbsr@gmail.com; Courtesy: Narthaki.com)

Making the most of the fact that his secret room is right beside the radio station's library, he spends his free waking hours there, again, 'listening, listening'.

'My duty was to give the music to the artistes who came to sing, and in the process, I learnt to arrange music for the interludes, and compose too. I learnt Oriya very quickly, because no one spoke Hindi. Soon, people started thinking I was an Oriya too.'

Two aspects of Hariprasad's talent must have inspired the next turn in his musical career.

As the only flautist among instrumentalists, he is often asked to join in as accompanist. And soon enough, the tonal quality of his flute, his long, sustained playing style and his eagerness to take up every opportunity make him a regular in the recording room. A facet that enhances his practice as well as his exposure to the music of his contemporaries.

The second, more important fact is Krishnamurthy's ability to see his ward's latent genius.

Hariprasad, as well as many other artistes who knew him or worked with him, are eloquent about Krishnamurthy's contribution to classical music and their own careers. 'He gave me a free hand,' Hariprasad says, adding that he was even allowed to use the studios for riyaz.

Krishnamurthy could understand the impact music could have in anyone's life. It was a driving force in his own, after all. Over and above his duties as station director, he would compose music and conduct the orchestra himself. Multitalented as an instrumentalist, he would play pieces on the keyboard to demonstrate. Other times, he would hum the tune or play the rhythm on the ghatam, which he had learnt during his tutelage in Carnatic music, in earlier years.

'He was sent to me by God,' Hariprasad says simply. He remembers the casual way the door opened to the path that would lead to the next turning point in his career. 'Krishnamurthy asked me to join his orchestra. In the beginning, I played short interlude pieces, filling in the gaps,' the maestro's eyes twinkle as he adds, 'but soon the pieces became longer.'

Word of mouth spreads now of his prowess, and what the flute adds to the compositions, and soon the flautist is on demand practically incessantly. It is a portent of things to come.

Knowing the time is right, Krishnamurthy suggests Hariprasad audition for the composer category. With his instinctive aplomb, the legend-in-the-making sails through. He now has a licence to compose, and lends his talent wherever it is needed in composing light tunes.

He is one more milestone closer to where his ultimate goal awaits.

Prafulla Kar is a music director of renown in Orissa. His home in Bhubaneswar is a showcase of the many awards and honours his work has won him. A painting of Lata Mangeshkar has pride of place; the musician is also a painter and this, he admits, is his quiet tribute to the Nightingale's genius. In the early 1960s, Kar was a junior practising law, but music was his passion. Like many others of his time forced to follow a 'decent' profession, he would toil over legal cases by day, except when summoned to perform at the radio station. 'I would go as a casual artiste, at twenty rupees for a programme, and Hari was already employed there. We often performed together, and got friendly.'

Kar's musical lineage is impressive. His uncle (father's elder brother), Khetra Mohan Kar, was a national-level tabla player, while he himself holds a Visharad in music and has innumerable awards, including the Padma Shri, to his credit.

'Hari's designation was of a player, but he often composed, even before he became a staff composer,' Kar recounts. He remembers a song sung by Mohammad Sikandar Alam, an artiste two years his senior, '*Sagore adhira nira taranga*', composed by Hariprasad. 'I never sang his compositions, though,' he clarifies.

Kar paints a picture of the halcyon days of youth when they were budding creative artistes. 'We used to meet at Bakshi Bazaar crossing, at the chowk, which was a meeting place of artists, singers, writers, lyricists. There was a paan shop there, Kisu (his name was Kishen Bhagat) Paan Dukaan. His paan was very popular, it had handmade tobacco in it. We call it *gundi* in Oriya. That was our adda.

'I loved the paan so much, I smuggled it in, tobacco and all, when I went to Austria, Russia,' he adds in an aside.

'The shop opposite would shut,' he recalls, 'and we would congregate in its verandah around 6 o'clock every evening. We would chat, argue, and, if there were any visits made to the country liquor shop nearby, there would even be some fights. Hari was not very regular, but would come on and off, till he left Cuttack. He would share his creations, I would share a new tune . . . and we would have creative interactions. Hari was mostly self-taught. Yet, his compositions were all raga-based even then. He would adapt and innovate. I thought he was very intelligent, very talented. Few of the others realized the depth of his talent.'

Kar remembers that when he went to Bombay for a recording, 'Hari sent sweets in bulk for Bhubaneswar. I learnt humanity from him, that if you give love, you get love. While hate only breeds hate.'

Opportunities to perform now came his way thick and fast. Hariprasad made the most of them all.

Ensemble piece, solo performances and compositions, and accompaniment requests for dancers in Odissi would follow one after the other. Krishnamurthy and Pt Mishra were already collaborating with Odissi Guru Kelucharan Mohapatra, and Hariprasad would be a vital part of the orchestra, adding his notes wherever he could fit them in. Poet Jayadeva's *Geet Govind*, describing the relationship between Krishna and Radha, as well as with the gopis of Vrindavan, was often a bulwark of the Odissi pieces choreographed by Guru Mohapatra and was actually incomplete without Krishna's flute playing through the composition. Hariprasad filled the gap admirably.

It is not long before Hariprasad finds himself forming the third component of a trio, along with Krishnamurthy and Guru Kelucharan, working with them on creating and playing music for the guru's new dance drama ballet creations.

Soon, other dance institutions take note, and requests start coming in for him to add the plaint of the flute to the rhythm of the pakhavaj, tabla and ghungroo and the cadences of the singer's voice.

And at every opportunity, Hariprasad presents himself as a willing accompanist.

Now, he is also a full-fledged composer. He creates his first offering as a composer. It is to be an Oriya song. The words are 'Aaji Paho na Rati', and singer Shyamal Mitra will give it voice. It is in many ways a big break for the flautist–composer. Mitra was a singer on par with Hemant Kumar and Manna Dey in the Bengali film fraternity. A composer in his own right, Mitra had many Bangla films to his credit and would go on to contribute to Hindi cinema too, including hits in *Amanush* and *Ananda Ashram*.

Unfazed by the celebrity status of his singer, Hariprasad delineates the tune to him in the studio. He then takes his place as flautist in the orchestra, as the recording begins.

Mitra's voice and perfect Oriya enunciation combined with Hariprasad's dulcet composition creates waves. Radio stations across Orissa pick up and relay the song, and critics are alerted to a new star on the rise among composers of music.

Stage performance requests dovetail one another, and our talented artiste is now found performing frequently not just in Cuttack, but at music festivals in Sambhalpur, and elsewhere. He remembers the feeling of familiarity that engulfed him, when on his way to a performance in Calcutta, he got off the train at Howrah and heard the cries of the hawkers at the platform, identical to what he had heard on his very first trip to Cuttack. The modest programme would result in a meeting with the 'great Amir Khan sahab'. 'He said he had come to listen to me, can you believe that?' Hariprasad exclaims.

Surjit Singh writes in detail about one of Hariprasad's earliest programmes in Cuttack. To quote from *Woodwinds of Change*:

The programme was organized by a Calcuttan and was held in a large hall about twenty kilometres from Bhubaneswar. The list of performers read like a who's who of classical musicians. Baba Allauddin Khan, Ravi Shankar, Ali Akbar Khan and Kanan sahib were among the participants. Someone suggested that Hariprasad play the flute as there were no flautists.

Hariprasad realizes this is his big chance. Here, among the greats, for the first time, he will play classical music to an audience, unlike the light pieces he played on radio. Yet, the event robs him of sleep at night—the thought of being on the same stage as the stalwarts sends the adrenaline rushing into his blood. Baba Allauddin Khan sahab! He remembers the kindly elder with crinkling eyes, the smell of his bidi. He cannot fall short of his expectations. He must prepare for the concert.

Hariprasad remembers that he retired to his favourite nook, the radio station library, and listened endlessly to the greats he was soon to meet. He listened to other singers and instrumentalists too.

'I wanted to understand how each developed his unique style, I wanted a style of my own,' he says.

When he was finally done with this exercise, he looked for a vacant studio, closed the door and practised, unmindful of the hours slipping quietly past. He only emerged when it was time for the evening broadcasts, tired but happy, his sweat-soaked shirt sticking to his torso.

Of the actual performance Hariprasad only says that he was overwhelmed by the fact that the venerable Ustad Karmatullah Khan accompanied him in a gesture of infinite grace. He has little recollection of the ragas he played, but remembers playing them with full gusto to impress the luminaries present.

Unlike many bosses, Krishnamurthy aided his staffer in his escapades. 'He would tell me to sign the muster for the coming fifteen days in advance, if I was going to be absent and out of town,' Hariprasad says. 'In fact, as time passed, I was more out of the radio station than in it.'

The stints at the radio station are useful in nurturing his continued learning process, and in the fact that he meets luminaries from faraway Bombay. At one such recording, he plays for a song sung by Talat Mahmood. Perhaps, it is these interactions with the likes of Talat and Shyamal Mitra that ignite in the flautist the desire to expand his universe and dream of being part of the glittering world of Hindi playback music. He holds the dream close, wrapped up in a secret, sacred space in his mind, to be unwrapped and examined when he is dropping off to sleep. It is only a dream. His one mad trip to Bombay has told him how difficult it is to even enter a studio. But, as he tells himself, there is no harm in dreaming.

Not in his wildest dreams does he think that it is here, at the radio station, that a vital part of his future awaits him. Unknown to him, destiny is knitting the pattern that will form the backdrop of his life in the years to come. But there is time still, and our hero lives on unaware.

Like the other, divine player of the flute who captivated the minds of countless youngsters who were ready to abandon work and home simply to listen to him, Hariprasad, too, was soon surrounded by young women. Odissi dancers who would come begging for him to play for their performances. Among them one, who watching him surrounded thus, would, much like Radha, burn with unexpressed angst.

Angurbala Ray would have grown up in Jamshedpur in a palatial home with large echoing rooms filled with ornate, carved furniture pieces and endless corridors tastefully lined with oils and tapestries, had not the family been wrecked by ill fortune. 'Everything was under litigation, so my father took up a managerial job in a shipping company.'

Music was a constant, and an antidote to sadness over lost wealth and status, and the young girl grew up listening to her father sing bhajans in Oriya, or playing the tabla in his spare time. 'My father wanted me to learn classical music, and so I started learning to sing,' she says simply.

Angurbala is today better known as Anuradha, and is held in high esteem in the music community, not just owing to her status as the wife of Pt Hariprasad Chaurasia, but because of her own knowledge of classical music. Besides, it is a rather well-known fact that it is Anuradha Chaurasia who has been a constant anchor in her husband's life, helping him to steer his career towards his destiny.

Hariprasad remembers Anuradha as one of the singers who came to the studio on a regular basis to sing. She had a sweet voice, was well-versed in the ragas, and was at that time studying in Cuttack.

'I learnt music from many gurus,' Anuradha recounts. 'Music was one of my subjects at the D.M. Madan Girls' High School in Jamshedpur. I remember JRD would often come there with Ratan Tata. Our music teacher was Paresh Banerjee, and I was one of his pet pupils. I would participate in the Bengal Club/Utkal Association music competitions, and win prizes in both bhajan and thumri categories. I would go to listen to Allauddin Khan when he came to sing at the Bengal Club. My father carried home all the cups I won in school, and when, during the Education Week competitions, I came first, he realized that I could do something serious in music.'

Soon, the young student was learning from Ustad Firoz Khan. 'My father disregarded the clicking tongues and shaking heads of his conservative relatives about my learning from a Muslim, and let me continue with Ustad Firoz Khan,' she says. The teacher would share his knowledge with her for ten years, till she moved to Cuttack to join college.

'My father wanted me to go to Bade Ghulam Ali Khan sahab and learn from him, but the singer was ill, and refused to take me on. So I joined Shailabala Women's College in Cuttack.'

Cuttack would change the direction of Angurbala's life in many ways. For one, it would lead her away from classical music.

'A distant uncle, Kavichandra Kalicharan Patnaik, had heard me singing and had suggested I join college in Cuttack and learn Oriya music from him. It seemed a good idea.'

Patnaik was indeed as good as his word. He saw in his young singer niece the perfect partner to promote his cause.

In an impassioned blog on *Odisha Story,* an online news portal dedicated to Orissa, Shyamanuja Das[2] laments the fact that his state barely remembers Kavichandra Kalicharan Patnaik, the man who was instrumental in giving Oriya music and literature a distinct place among other art forms.

---

[2] Shyamanuja Das can be reached at shyamanuja@gmail.com. Courtesy: odishastory.com

And indeed, most of the core research for the lobbying for Oriya at the Sangeet Natak Akademi, which was taken up by other luminaries from Orissa, was spearheaded and undertaken by Patnaik.

To quote from the blog and showcase a crusader's work may be quite justified here. Das presents a brief overview of the nearly forgotten champion's contribution:

He worked with various groups to create the standard postures and rules of modern Odissi dance.

He visited different conferences to establish that Odissi, as music, is not just classical but is very different from both Hindustani and Carnatic music.

He named Odissi. David Denen, an American scholar, who has done extensive research on [the] naming of Odissi, has concluded, after referring to half a dozen scholars, that it was Kalibabu who named Odissi. And the name itself was a master stroke. Not only did it secure its Odia connection forever, but it also created a classical aura for it, which would not have been [there] in a generic adjective like Odia.

It is his powerful lecture, accompanied by [a] demo, that convinced everyone, including famous Indologist and dance critic Dr Charles Fabri, that Odissi is a classical dance form. Indrani Rahman worked closely with him and was trained by his disciple, Guru Deba Prasad Das.

He established the modern theatre culture in Odisha. His Odisha Theatres was the first professional theatre group in Odisha.

He was the first to experiment with modern themes in theatre and music. A playwright and lyricist par excellence, he wrote on traditional themes as well as contemporary social themes and popularized them.

He was a pioneer in modern recorded music from Odisha. He himself and his protégé Sumati Devi recorded a number of songs for HMV.

His association with early Odia films is a subject in itself. He not only wrote lyrics for many early movies such as *Lalita*, *Rolls-28*, *Kedar Gouri* and *Dasyu Ratnakar*, he also scored music in one movie, *Naari*. His association with Odia cinema continued well into the '60s, when he wrote for movies such as *Manika Jodi*, *Ghara Bahuda* and *Kie Kahara*, the second movie for Akshaya Mohanty as a composer. He wrote the story for *Rolls-28*, script for *Jayadeba* and co-directed and acted in *Naari*.

Some of the songs written by him, such as '*Asa jibana dhana mora pakhala kansaa*' (sung by both Balakrushna Dash and Shyamamani Devi) are milestones in [the] popularity of Odia palligeeti.

He even dabbled with recording in Odisha by establishing a recording company in Cuttack.

He tried his hand at publishing a full-fledged music journal, probably the only such journal ever to be published in Odia.

His direct disciples and protégés—Sumati Devi and Angurbala in music, Deba Prasad Das and Indrani Rahman in dance, and actors such as Samuel Sahu (Babi), Priyanath Mishra (Pira) and Gloria Mohanty who excelled in theatre and cinema—too contributed immensely to their respective fields.

Taking charge of the young collegian, Mahapatra started cleaning up her enunciation of the Oriya language as the first step to learning its music. Soon, she was taking lessons from him in Oriya music.

'At that time, Oriya music and dance were not considered part of the Indian classical tradition, and my father as well as my guru were very upset by my change of track. They felt I was losing my classical base. "What I taught you was classical, and now look at you," Firoz Khan said.'

His pupil never met her estranged teacher after that, as he passed away.

However, his teaching stood her in good stead and she proved a quick learner who was soon a skilled exponent of Oriya music.

As part of a small group moving across the state to popularize art forms, Angurbala accompanied her uncle to give demonstrations. Perhaps, as much to be near his daughter as to steer her back into classical singing, she observes, 'My father took voluntary retirement and shifted to Patia near Cuttack in the following year. However, he passed away within a year. I got my mom to Orissa; she did not stay in Cuttack, but at our ancestral place 20 km away. My two sisters and brother were with her too.'

'I was a college student when I made acquaintance with him,' Anuradha says, reminiscing about her early meetings with Hariprasad. 'I had heard him play, and realized there was something exceptional in the quality of his music.' Anuradha does not elaborate on when she first realized she was attracted to the flautist, but the unspoken is evident when she says, 'I wanted him to play for me, but he was always surrounded. I had my own ego issues, so I kept out of the melee.'

But meetings seemed inevitable. Hariprasad often visited her college to play as accompanist to the college dance troupes which boasted of future stars, including Sanjukta Panigrahi and Kumkum Mohanti. Angurbala was part of the same group of accompanists, in the role of a singer. Rehearsals were regular, and meeting face-to-face, inevitable. 'Eventually, a friendship developed between us. When I shifted from the hostel to my uncle's place, he would drop in to visit me.'

Anuradha also mentions her teaming up with Hariprasad during the Durga Puja broadcasts from the radio station. 'The courtship intensified when I was in the third year of college. I enrolled for a

BA in music at the Kala Vikas Kendra where Khitish Mitra was a professor, but missed Firoz Khan sahab's teaching.'

It was inevitable that the small community they moved about in would notice that the singer and flautist were keeping more company than a professional association demanded, and soon there were reactions from Angurbala's family. The objections were the usual tried-and-tested ones of caste, region, language. Moreover, Hariprasad was a musician, and therefore suspected of easy philandering ways. An accusation that, despite his popularity with the Odissi dancers, was quite far from the truth.

Unable to find the gumption to fly openly in the face of such disapproval, Hariprasad and Angurbala got married secretly. Anuradha recounts, 'We married against the will of our relatives, at a temple, on 15 August 1958. The only person I could ask for help was Prof. Nityanand Durzee who had often told me to follow my heart and not think of caste or creed. I was learning philosophy from him. His mother helped me through the secret ceremony.'

Their trials as a couple should have ended with that step towards mutual commitment, but there were storms brewing ahead.

'They transferred him to Bombay AIR,' says Anuradha simply.
In hindsight, the statement has lost its sting. But when he first receives the order telling him he must leave Cuttack and report to work at the Bombay AIR station, the newlyweds are devastated. Their little, secret paradise is shattering even before they have had time to set it up.

Surjit Singh hints at office politics as the cause. Other artistes complaining about Hariprasad's long and frequent absenteeism could well have been a trigger. There was also the fact that seeing his niece, so vital to his cause of promoting Oriya culture, was drifting away, swayed by love for a man who did not even belong to the same class or region, must have perturbed Kalicharan Patnaik considerably. Whether the uncle played a hand in the transfer, as a move to separate his niece from her beau's influence and to get her back as chief assistant in his own crusade, is a matter of conjecture. The undeniable fact is that Krishnamurthy had been transferred out of Cuttack, and a new station director now occupied the chair. He could not have but noticed that the lone flautist on the rolls spent more time out of the office than in it. Perhaps, as much to avoid a confrontation as to rid himself of an absentee musician, he summoned

Hariprasad to his cabin and told him that he should accept a transfer to Bombay. When the statement was met with silence from a stunned and uncomprehending Hariprasad, whose mind must have been trying to grapple with the manifold implications of the sentence just delivered, the station director told him that the only alternative to the transfer was to tender his resignation.

Sitting by himself in the room he now occupies in esraj artiste Bankim Pal's house, Hariprasad weighs the pros and cons of what he stands to lose if he accepts the transfer to Bombay. The thought has diminished his natural buoyancy, bringing him to despair. Now, he realizes, reason must be given a chance, and it is only sensible to see what lies ahead and weigh it against what he will lose when he leaves Cuttack.

His life here has been cocooned in music. Well ensconced in Oriya films, he has a successful, ongoing partnership with his one-time mentor, Bhubaneswar Mishra, creating music for Oriya films. The songs have won acclaim as well as a place in the hearts of listeners. Would his moving mean the end of this creative phase? Bombay was a giant megapolis, known both for being a cornucopia of opportunity as well as a cruel city that could, without a second thought, wipe out an aspirant.

Then there are the dancers in the many institutes who clamour for him to accompany them as an instrumentalist. It gives him great pleasure to know he is a vital part of the state's cultural evolution. And the money he earns is not to be ignored either.

But above all, and this is what is most heart-wrenching to him really, is the knowledge that he has no idea as to how he can get

Angurbala to join him in his new assignment. Not only is their marriage still under wraps, but she is caught in the thick of her exams . . .

Yet, once again, at a new crossroads, he finds himself packing his trunk. As he places his meagre clothes inside, one by one, he repeats the mantra that has worked for him in the past. One which his friends had also offered as advice. 'I will give it a chance for a month, and if it does not work, I will resign and return,' he tells himself.

Decision made, he feels lighter at heart again. The clouds still hover overhead, but he can see the silver lining.

Bombay

(1962 onwards)

He gets off the train at the awesome Victoria Terminus station in Bombay. The gothic building dwarfs everyone who passes through it, and Hariprasad, stepping into the busy, teeming city of dreams cannot but feel intimidated. It is the same feeling that engulfed him when he visited the place earlier. The fact that, unlike the many he sees around on the streets, he is not a wastrel, he has a job in hand with a government organization, gives him courage.

He reports to the AIR station at Churchgate, looking the prototype of the artiste, clad in dhoti and kurta, with a cloth bag slung on one shoulder to hold his flute and documents. The sounds from the studios do not reach his ears yet, as he waits to be assigned his duties. 'Nothing much happened on the first day of work,' he recalls.

No airy room awaits him, and he pushes away the memory of the sweet cottage his earlier workplace had offered. 'It was not at all easy,' Hariprasad remembers wryly. 'Within the first fifteen days, I felt I would fall sick.'

He takes up accommodation with his sister, Banno, who lives further north, in Bhuleshwar, but still close enough for him to commute to work. In Banno's house too, strapped as the family is for space in a city where living space remains among the highest priced in the world, Hariprasad is consigned to the balcony.

But the silver lining continues to shine, growing brighter still. He discovers that the artistes who walk through the long corridors of the radio station include some of the greats in the music world, among them music directors. He hears their names mentioned . . . Anil Biswas, S.N. Tripathi. And there are others who are commissioned to create and compose for radio. Here again is an opportunity to listen and learn, for he believes learning should never stop. So he listens. And as he goes about his duties, which are nowhere as exciting as his work in Cuttack had been, he still finds enough in the music of others to entertain and enlighten himself. And who knows, maybe one day, one of them would welcome him into the mysterious and dazzling world of Hindi films!

There is after all, he tells himself, no harm in dreaming.

Opportunity favours the true of heart. He makes friends easily anyway, and shares with them his dreams, his fierce love of music. Bombaywallas are renowned for living private lives: the long commutes most find they must necessarily undertake, and the mixed bag of communities the city throws together, make almost every man an island unto himself. Yet, there are exceptions. Hariprasad finds one such in Ahmed Darbar, who also works at the radio station. One thing leads to another, and soon our flautist is busy every evening, playing his flute through the two-hour-long Gujarati plays directed and produced by Irani seth (Faridun Irani), for whom Darbar moonlights, composing the music. Hariprasad does not know it then, but he is not the only one dreaming. Irani's daughter, Aruna, too dreams of a role in Hindi films, and eagerly auditions at studios by day, returning in time for make-up before taking up her role on stage in the evening.

Hari-ji believes it was one of his morning renditions over the radio that changed his fortunes forever.

'One day, the studio got a call asking for Hariprasad Chaurasia, flute player,' he recounts. 'So I am called to the phone, and I take the receiver and lift it to my ear wondering who it can be, hoping it is not bad news. The voice at the other end introduces itself as Master Sonik. "Can you come to the studio?" he wants to know. I am surprised. But I understand that he is an assistant with the music director Madan Mohan, and they are waiting to record, but their flautist has not come. And they want me to go there. I say, "I don't know my way, I am new," and he tells me he will pick me up. I was of course keen to meet music directors. I heard Lata-ji was singing the song . . . I went.

'When I entered the studio, all turned to look at me in my dhoti and kurta. I got nervous. Many of the instrumentalists were obviously Christians, wearing pants and shirts. They stared at me. Then I was asked to play. I played my flute. Lata-ji was there, she looked at me when she heard the sound. Perhaps she recognized the sound.'

It was not the first time Hariprasad was entering a recording studio that was recording for a film. Often, in his interviews, he has said that the first song he recorded was for Lata Mangeshkar, who sang 'Main to tum sangh nain milayke, har gayi sajna' from *Man Mauji*, a song whose tune he remembers well enough to hum too. But that recording was much earlier, during a previous trip when he had come with other Oriya artistes to record an Oriya song. He had interacted with the singer then, whom he admired hugely, and asked her for advice on how to join the industry. Then, recording over, the group had gone back.

This time, the orchestra he takes his place in will support not Lata Mangeshkar, as he had hoped, but singer Talat Mahmood as he sings a ghazal. The film is *Jahan Ara*, which would be released in 1964. Based on Emperor Shah Jahan's daughter, it weaves a story around the sacrifice of her love so she can look after her father thanks to a promise she has given her dying mother. Bharat Bhushan, star of many historicals and films centred on musical legends, plays the role of Mirza, the thwarted lover who expresses his pain through some of Madan Mohan's sweetest compositions with lyrics by Rajinder Krishen.

The song that is being recorded is one such plaint . . . '*Phir wohi shaam*'.

If Hariprasad looked towards the singer who had also turned to see the flautist coming in, and hoped that Talat Mahmood would recognize him, his hope was belied. They had met during a recording, when the singer had recorded an Oriya song at the Cuttack radio station, and Mahmood had remarked on the quality of the flautist's playing, adding that he should try to come to Bombay and find a place in the orchestra in films. 'I could see he had no memory of having met me,' Hariprasad says of this second encounter.

But there is no time to ponder over the past. It is time to rehearse and record. 'Master Sonik gave me my cue sheet with my part in it, and asked, "Can you follow this?" I said yes. And we started.'

The flute comes in right at the prelude to the song, '*Phir wohi shaam*'. It continues to play softly almost right through, intermittently adding pathos to the singer's voice as he laments over his loneliness without his beloved. In the interludes, it is sometimes heard singly before it blends in with the rest of the orchestra. 'I played wherever I felt the mood was right and my flute was needed,' Hariprasad says, reminiscing about that first recording.

A lesser artiste might have earned a rebuke for straying from the score sheet. But such is the tenor of his playing that the music director takes notice. 'After the recording, Madan Mohan said, "Let him stay back. He must be present at every session, whether or not he is required." I think my playing was a sensation, something new,' he adds, eyes twinkling at the memory.

Just to mention a coincidence, Aruna Irani, whom Hariprasad saw most evenings on stage in her father's theatre production, also had a role in *Jahan Ara*. And, some years later, Master Sonik would form his own music team with his nephew Omi, and they would compose for films under the name Sonik–Omi. Among them were *Dil Ne Phir Yaad Kiya* and *Mahua*. Hariprasad's flute would find place in most of their compositions.

It was not unusual for classical musicians to be part of the orchestra playing for film songs. In fact, even well-known, much respected singers from venerable gharanas were sometimes persuaded to lend their voice for celluloid. As early as 1952, Naushad had persuaded D.V. Paluskar, son of the venerable father of the Gandharva Mahavidyalayas and the architect of formalized music education in India, to sing for *Baiju Bawra*. It was no mean feat, as the young Paluskar was perhaps the only musician to achieve national fame as a gifted classical singer by the age of twenty. The song '*Aaj gawat man mero jhoomke*', a duet in Raga Desi, sung by an equally respected classical singer, Amir Khan, pitted a celluloid Baiju against the court poet, Tansen, and remains one of the true gems among classical songs in cinema.

Three years later, V. Shantaram would persuade Amir Khan to sing for his dance-based extravaganza, *Jhanak Jhanak Payal Baje*. With lyrics by Hasrat Jaipuri set to tune by Vasant Desai, the song was used in the opening credits of the film. Shantaram would repeat the idea by getting the reclusive Kishori Amonkar to sing the title song for his 1964 film, *Geet Gaya Patharon Ne*.

Yet again, in 1960, Naushad persuaded director K. Asif and the producer of *Mughal-e-Azam,* Shapoorji Pallonji, to recruit the inimitable Bade Ghulam Ali Khan to sing as Tansen, a feat that was made possible when the producer agreed to the humongous fee of 25,000 rupees demanded by the singer, which he thought would deter the producer and the composer. The normal range of payment for a song at that time was 250 to 1000 rupees. The song, 'Shubh din aayo', is perhaps forgotten, but the scene it formed a backdrop to remains in the annals of film history as one of the most sensually romantic ever filmed.

Many classically trained instrumentalists too played in film music orchestras; it helped them earn more than their stage performances did. Ustad Raes Khan was one such sitarist, who, before he migrated to Pakistan to join his fourth wife, Bilqees Khanum, played for composer Madan Mohan for many of his compositions, perhaps the best known among them for use of the sitar being 'Nainon mein badara chhaye', from the film Mera Saaya.

Hariprasad would meet the famous sitarist at his very first recording for Jahan Ara.

Word travels quickly in industry circles. New talent, be it an actor or a musician, is immediately noticed, and eagerly signed on. Hariprasad soon finds out that he is the new sensation. 'Everybody wanted me,' he says simply.

'Everybody' included the music directors coming to the studio to compose background music and conduct, a phalanx of famous names in music direction. 'Soon, I was playing for every one of them, my diary was full. O.P. Nayyar, S.D. Burman, C. Ramchandra, Vasant Desai, Kalyanji–Anandji, Madan Mohan, of course, Shankar–Jaikishen, Laxmikant–Pyarelal . . . I was shuttling between recording rooms. Besides this, they were asking me to compose background music because they realized I was good at creating the right mood.'

He is earning more money now than his job gives him. If he is busy, it is with what he loves best, his music. The appreciation and welcome he gets everywhere are balm to his mind, boosting his confidence even further.

Soon he is able to think about putting his life on track. Gauging that Angurbala's examinations must be over, he decides to bring her to Bombay. As a self-made, cash-rich creative artiste, he has no need to take anyone's permission any more. He will lead his own life, the way he wants to.

He senses that his extracurricular musical work can get him into trouble with his bosses yet again. Already, friends at the station have alerted him to the fact that a few complaints have been registered against him. Hariprasad decides to resign as soon as possible. He also moves out of Banno's house, where there is no space for an extra person, and takes up a room in Evergreen Hotel near Khar railway station.

'He came to fetch me, and I left with him for Bombay,' Anuradha says. In that sentence is encapsulated the momentous feeling that she has stepped into a new world, and a new life.

Evergreen Hotel still exists in Khar. Few who go past it, hurrying to or from the station on whatever task they have on hand, stop to look at it. Its exteriors do not hold any indication of the dreams of the many luminaries its rooms must once have nurtured, or of the creative moments and happy memories it must have been home to.

The search engine yahoo.com announces that Hotel Evergreen, 'has 22 rooms, spread across 4 floors. Each room has an attached bathroom with hot and cold water supply. The in-room amenities include a wardrobe and cable TV. This Mumbai hotel provides room, laundry, and medical services. It houses a restaurant and has a backup generator facility. The hotel operates a 24-hour front desk and also a tour desk.'

In the 1960s, though, it was a much humbler version, which, perhaps due to its proximity to the railway station and because it is in what was then a faraway suburb close enough to the studios, attracted a lot of those who waited to get their big break while they made do with whatever came their way by way of work in films. Anand Bakshi and S.D. Burman were among those who had stopped here, birds on their way to more splendorous destinations.

'I was in a room the size of a train compartment,' Hariprasad remembers. 'It was a busy hotel, and everyone was busy too.'

Among his earliest memories of life at Hotel Evergreen is one that still evokes a smile on his face. 'I would spend the mornings doing riyaz,' he says. 'The first time, when I was practising long alaaps, Iftekhar, who also lived there, came running. "What is it!" he asked, breathless, anxious. "Is someone dead?"'

He remembers Anand Bakshi who was there at the same time, besides Iftekhar and his wife.

Anuradha's memory is sharper. 'Besides Burman dada and Anand Bakshi, Manubhai Vakil was there with his family; his daughter Rupa and I became good friends. The choreographer, Sharma, was living there too. A single room cost 125 rupees. It would have been impossible on his salary of 250, but his outside income was by now substantial. I bought a small stove and used to cook dal-chawal in the room for us.'

Anuradha, a small-town girl still new to the city, would gawk at Madhubala whenever she drove up to Hotel Evergreen. 'She was friendly with Iftekhar's wife, a Jewish girl, and I would stand at the railing and stare at her whenever she came to visit!'

The young couple owned almost nothing. 'All our belongings were in a small trunk,' Anuradha says. 'I had no jewellery, only two gold bangles . . . and that too got stolen. While he was with the radio station, I would stand in the balcony waiting for him to return. I had imagined life very differently, [I'd] thought, in Bombay, I would meet heroes and heroines. I had planned to work, and between the salary I earned and his work with the radio station, we would live modestly. But he was never there. It got worse once he left his job.'

As Hariprasad got increasingly busy, Anuradha began to feel what most wives left at home by busy husbands feel—loneliness, and a sense of emptiness. There was no doubt about the fact that her husband had little time for anything beyond work. It was left to Anuradha to ensure her husband looked presentable when he went to work. 'She would shop for me, buy the clothes and whatever else I needed. I was just too busy,' Hariprasad says.

'I once worked fifteen days at a stretch, day and night,' Hariprasad remembers. 'The morning shift would start at 10 o'clock and I would play for the songs that were being recorded through the day, often shuttling from one studio to another. At night, my second shift would begin,' he says with a smile, 'and I would work on background scores. I would carry a toothbrush in my pocket, some gum and my packet of paan, and catch a nap once the night recording was over. Then be ready by 10 to start again.'

'Money came in very fast,' Anuradha remembers, 'his pockets would be stuffed with notes that he would empty out on the bed. He would not even have counted it, he just did not have the time. Then he would start getting ready to rush out again. It was unending.'

In the NCPA interview, Hariprasad's face takes on the expression of a child showing off the trophy he has won, when he tells his interviewer, accomplished sitarist Arvind Parikh, 'I was soon playing for songs in all languages. I would play in Calcutta in the morning, be playing in Bombay in the afternoon, and play at a recording in Gemini Studios, Madras, the same night . . . Everyone wanted me, so I went.'

To keep her growing despondency over her absentee husband at bay, Anuradha returned to music. After all, she was a singer of no mean talent herself. Ramesh Nadkarni, who had earlier been at AIR Cuttack, was also with the radio station in Bombay, now as producer, and he started teaching her. Anuradha rues the fact that she 'never got around to auditioning or singing publicly, as I developed a thyroid problem, which thickened my voice. After that, I restricted my singing to inside my home.'

Other avenues were also not offering much hope. Studying for a master's in philosophy in Bombay in the English medium for someone who has had most of her education in Hindi, can prove challenging, and Anuradha found herself not quite up to the challenge. She completed the course, 'though it took three years, instead of two'.

Anuradha remembers it was in the year Pt Jawaharlal Nehru died that they left Hotel Evergreen.

When Hariprasad realizes they have enough money to set up a home of their own, the Chaurasias move into Shiv Darshan, on the ground floor, on 20th road, Khar. The two-room-kitchen has a much coveted balcony, and costs them '10,000 rupees as pagree and 250 rupees a month as rent'.

Like S.D. Burman, Hariprasad also gets himself a car. While the music director invests in a Fiat, our flautist falls in love with a Morris Eight. He has by now got a friend to teach him to drive, and plans to zoom about in his dinky four-wheeler. He had not known it till then, but owning a car seemed to unleash a sense of power as well as a latent love of automobiles. As Anuradha puts it, 'Once he got rid of the Morris, which did give a lot of trouble, he kept buying cars. We have owned by turn an Ambassador, Triumph, Fiat, Austin Cambridge, Mercedes . . . he used to drive, expertly, and has driven all over the world whenever he got the opportunity.'

Indeed, Hariprasad was playing in three cities. The flute has no language; it is the voice of pure music. Regardless of the language of the lyrics of a song, the flute could lend its own meanings and overtones, adding to the melancholy of the song, or celebrating its joyousness, as required.

Although he plays for countless films made in the south, it is K. Viswanath's Telugu film, *Sirivennela*, meaning moonlight, made in 1986, that he remembers sharply. Perhaps because the hero of the film is not only a flautist, but also named Hariprasad, a blind, but gifted singer and flute player whose art wins for him the love of two women, as well as the honorific of Pandit.

Viswanath was known for his path-breaking themes, including casteism and alcoholism. He was able to make films that teased out the emotions of the audience sufficiently enough to make them remember the themes and images vividly. More important, the filmmaker who received innumerable awards for his films is also credited with one of them, *Sankarabharanam*, being instrumental in reviving an interest in Carnatic music in the generation that viewed the film.

In *Sirivennela*, Viswanath explored the world of visually and aurally impaired people. Giving his protagonist mastery over the flute automatically meant that no other than the talented Bombay-based flautist could play the instrument for the film. Spreading his net wide, the director had signed on Bangla actors—Sarvadaman Banerjee for the main role and Moon Moon Sen as his love interest, along with Suhasini Mani Ratnam as the silent lover who pines for the hero.

According to Hariprasad, 'The music gave me enough scope to play not only in the song numbers but also right through the background of the film.' The film went on to win awards, but the classical music scores composed by H.K.V. Mahadevan and embellished by Hariprasad resound even today, and are counted among music lovers' all-time favourites.

Woodwinds of Change records another memory Hariprasad has shared with its author, of a Malayalam film, *Pokkuveyil* (Twilight), where he composed the music. The film, made in 1982, before *Sirivennela*, by the noted director, (late) G. Aravindan, was experimental and centred on the hero, a flautist, who, thanks to being alienated, feels despair and succumbs to mental illness. 'When Aravindan first discussed the music with Hariprasad, it was to be a soundtrack consisting of his flute only. No percussion, no vocals, not even the drone of a tanpura; just unconnected pieces of flute music that would inspire Aravindan to *compose* scenes around it,' Surjit Singh writes.

However, the flautist added the tabla and the sarod. At the studio, he was asked to 'just play'. He did, and in two hours, the entire score was ready. When the film received good reviews and was a hit, Hariprasad received flowers from the happy director.

When it came to Bangla films, Salil Chowdhury was one among the music directors who sought his talent in their compositions. Hariprasad talks of Hemant Kumar taking him to Calcutta for *Balika Bodhu*. He still remembers the picture of a very young Moushumi in bridal attire, playing the teenaged bride; he notes that her face has the childlike innocence that makes her perfect for the part. Hemant Kumar and Hariprasad have had occasions to interact; as singer and instrumentalist, they have listened to each other across studios, recorded songs for S.D. Burman and others. A much-loved music director himself, Hemant Kumar has enough clout in his hometown to demand that the flautist of his choice be flown down from Bombay for his film. 'In Calcutta, Pahari Sanyal and others would come to the studio to listen to me,' he says. 'I could not believe it!'

The link with Hemant Kumar would extend beyond film music. Hemant-da, as the industry knew him, would be the one to take Hariprasad on his very first trip overseas, in 1966. Hariprasad would not only accompany the singer, as would others, along with the tabla of course, but would also render a solo piece to acquaint foreign audiences with the virtuosity of the humble instrument.

It would not be long before the soft-spoken artiste whose twinkling eyes spoke of his ready sense of humour would win over audiences around the globe, thanks to his dexterity with the simple bamboo instrument of his choice.

An Interlude

London. 1966. It is a strange world he finds himself in. For one, he is cold. His hands are cold, his fingers too, as is the tip of his nose. Worst of all, his flute is not warm and responsive to his touch, but feels cold. He lifts it to his lips, blows tentatively; the sound comforts him, it is almost clear as always, except for the slightest hint of a hiss. Perhaps if he wraps the flute up in a woollen scarf, it will feel better . . .

He looks around at the hall he is to perform in. It is huge, and impressive. He has already been awed by the building's façade, but the semicircular seating inside, with tiers that rise one over the other in a widening arc, is like nothing he has seen before. He does not know if all the plush seats will be filled—there seem to be so many! He supposes it must be some thousands. (The actual number is 5267.)

His recital is part of an evening of dance and music. He has been asked to play for twelve minutes.

When his turn comes, the audience welcomes him with applause, as is the custom in the West. It warms his heart. He has decided to play a simple raga, knowing that the time allotted is not enough for anything complex. He looks into the dim interiors of the space before him, settles down, signals to the tabla player accompanying him, and closing his eyes, blows into his flute.

'When I play, I close my eyes, because then I am playing only for God.'

For the stretch of time that follows, he is aware of nothing except his music. He could well be sitting by Draupadi Ghat in Allahabad. Tabla and flute play in tandem, then together, in perfect sync, and listening to the music, the audience is in thrall. It knows it is in the presence of a true master.

When the recital ends, the clock shows that it has lasted twenty minutes. But the audience does not mind. It calls for an encore.

Flushed and happy, Hariprasad stands in the wings, waiting for the applause to stop. Someone pushes him on to the stage, telling him to take a bow. He stumbles out; then, walking up to centrestage, bends low in a namaste.

It is much later that he realizes the magnitude of his achievement. Not only has he performed at the Royal Albert Hall, London, coveted venue of every performing artiste across the world, but the audience of British and Indian listeners boasted celebrity performers, including Yehudi Menuhin, the world-famous violinist.

He celebrates by buying gifts for Anuradha. Perfumes, which, in those days, were not available as easily as they are now, in India.

On the home front, much has changed. Anuradha has found ways to gather the disparate segments of her husband's life together and knit them into a harmonious whole.

No one in the Chaurasia family denies that Hariprasad was married to Kamala. It was a match made by his father, and there was no question of disobedience. Kamala, a distant relative and a simple woman, would bear her husband two sons. When Hariprasad moved to Bombay, he left Kamala at his paternal home.

Anuradha does not like to talk about it, but records show that it was at her behest that Kamala and her two children travelled from Allahabad, where they lived in a house Hariprasad had bought for them and his father, to Khar. Unlike what it is in TV serials, where women prove to be one another's worst enemies, Hariprasad's wives found a feeling of sisterhood between them, and enjoyed each other's company. With Hariprasad busy all the time, it was a boon to have each other for company. When Kamala's boys were sent to good boarding schools, she found a conduit for her motherly love in Anuradha's baby, Rajeev, who was born when her older boy was almost ten years old, in 1968. Surjit Singh notes that Rajeev was 'all love for his mummy', a term he used to address both Kamala and

Anuradha. Surjit quotes Rajeev, adding, 'I miss her a lot. She died in 1988. When I was young, I always thought I would make a hospital or some such philanthropic institution in her name.' Singh adds that the flautist ensured that both his sons from Kamala were given a good education, that they completed their MBAs, and held good jobs. The families, he writes, would meet now and then, and spend a brief weekend together.

Anuradha would find another friend and companion in Manorama Sharma, the gifted and beautiful wife of Shivkumar Sharma.

Hariprasad and Shivkumar Sharma first met in the late 1950s, in Delhi.

Shivkumar remembers that it was at Talkatora Stadium, at an inter-collegiate meet. 'We met briefly, and got on well. I think it was in 1958 . . .'

Looking back, that inter-collegiate meet was a historic one indeed. The lives of such diverse personalities as Jagjit Singh, Subhash Ghai, Amjad Khan and Hariprasad Chaurasia are all marked by this milestone. Each of them was at the meet; each of them was chasing a dream. 'I was there representing my university in dramatics,' Subhash Ghai said in an interview for a biography of Jagjit Singh. 'Jagjit was there as a singer, and Amjad Khan was also in dramatics.'

Shivkumar Sharma was representing Jammu University, as tabla and santoor player in the instrumental category.

While Jagjit and Subhash struck up a friendship that would span their entire lifetime, another long-lived friendship did not spark off quite as brightly at the meet. Perhaps because, unlike the others who were representing universities, Hariprasad was at the event in the capacity of an accompanist. 'I was representing my college in the classical music section, and Hariprasad came along to accompany me on the flute,' Anuradha explains. 'Perhaps because he was not a college student like the others, he kept to himself.'

According to Shivkumar Sharma, 'We did not keep in touch, but met again, in the early 1960s, in a studio in Bombay.'

He had already learnt the truth about life in Bombay, trying to make his mark as a santoor player in an industry that had no ears for him.

He describes the journey that got him to the 'city of a thousand opportunities'. 'I was a bit of a rebel. I left home abruptly; it was a turning point in my life. I was running away from a nine-to-five job as a music producer at Ravenshaw College in Jammu. My father was head of the music section there. When I told my father this job was not for me, he confronted me, asking angrily what it was I wanted to do. "If you want to be a freelance musician, go somewhere where great musicians are and prove yourself," he taunted. I rose to the challenge. "I am leaving the day after tomorrow," I told him. He was surprised, he did not think I would take up the challenge, he asked me to wait and think it over. But I left. I remember the date, 1 June 1960.'

Destiny calls the talented to their goal. Bombay had become a gathering place for musical talents from all over the north. Music directors, singers, instrumentalists, all gravitated to the city, drawn by the steadily growing opportunities offered by the burgeoning film industry that promised work as well as glamour and fame.

Shivkumar Sharma had had a taste of the industry already, though by accident. Much in the same way that Hariprasad had played in the orchestra for the *Man Mauji* song by Lata Mangeshkar, a younger Shivkumar had made an 'accidental entry' in the background score of Shantaram's dance epic, *Jhanak Jhanak Payal Baaje*, and had even composed his own piece in it. In his words, he 'had come to Bombay to participate in the Haridas Sangeet Sammelan; the film was being made at that time, and somehow I ended up playing for it.'

Though he had stormed out of home and let his spirit of rebellion and urge to find his calling carry him all the way to Bombay, the young santoor player would find life in the city a struggle. 'I would often wonder if I should give up and leave.'

Everything changed when he ran into Hariprasad, when the flautist shifted to the city as composer, AIR, but was also recording at studios for film music.

'Our destinies were perhaps linked. We were both classically trained musicians who did not wish to remain studio recording musicians, but destiny had brought us there. It was a source of income, after all. Both of us were strugglers in our own way. We often had to face ridicule when we played at concerts. For one, my instrument was hardly known. Hari-ji was playing an instrument that was better known. Pannalal Ghosh had established it as a versatile instrument for music accompaniment, but Hari-ji was defying all known ways the flute was normally being played. He would change it further when he started learning from Annapurna-ji.

'In my case, whenever I played the santoor, reviewers would compare it with the sitar or the sarod, both of which were well established in classical music and much loved too. I had to fight for the santoor to find a place as an instrument capable of expressing classical music. Meanwhile, I kept myself afloat, courtesy film music.'

The second meeting between the two struggling classical instrumentalists had dramatic results. In Hariprasad, Shivkumar found 'the kind of friend who sustains you all through life'. Hariprasad also remembers that 'the chance meeting at Famous Studios developed into a friendship. We started meeting almost every day. We would talk about our music.' Anuradha adds, 'Often, the four of us would meet over dinner, or in free time, to just chat, laugh together or discuss our dreams.'

As friends, there would also be moments of fun and mischief.

Hariprasad tells the story well. 'One day, the bell rang. I was home, so opened the door. A young woman stood outside. She said namaste and added, "I have come for an interview with you." I looked at her. She had her head covered, there was fresh sindoor in the parting of her hair. I sensed mischief. I asked her, "Have you had your bath?" She looked at me confused and asked why. I said, "Because you look as if you have come straight from the station. Where is Shiv-ji hiding?" She tried to look surprised, but by then Shiv-ji had come out from behind the door, laughing.'

Manorama and Anuradha would form the perfect pair of wives of busy, dedicated musicians with fire in their belly to find their place in the world of classical music. Often left to themselves, they would seek each other's company and thus cement a friendship that lasts to this day.

The Film Years

(1981–1993)

In the short span of three years, Hariprasad has become a staple at recording studios across the country. No director composing for Bombay films can do without him; almost every song has an interlude by him. Even period films where the flute cannot be included in the music, find ways to add in a composition in the background score. Muzaffar Ali who directed one such movie remembers, 'When I started work on *Umrao Jaan*, I had got together musicians who were each a master at their art . . . people who believed in what they did. There was Hariprasad Chaurasia, Shivkumar Sharma, Zarine Daruwalla and her husband. Then there were Sultan Khan and Iqbal Khan on the sarangi, because in the film, everything started with and depended on the sarangi.'

Khayyam, who was composing the music for the film, was renowned for the fact that he would not let any singer deviate from the score, which he would hand out to each person in advance.

But Muzaffar managed to give the instrumentalists freedom in the background music. 'I would show them the edited scenes, and let them fill in the music. They would watch and realize there was only one way to fill it, and instinctively compose the best-suited tune, spin magic. Hariprasad, too, always knew exactly the length required.

He knew how to fill soul into the scene, draw out the right emotion from it. Hariprasad's flute comes in at softer moments, like towards the end of the film. Umrao is about to come face-to-face with her old home. In the first song, '*Kahe ko byahi bides*', his flute mingles beautifully with the shehnai, adding a new dimension to a traditional ditty. Of course, there are many more instances, but these come to mind right away.'

Umrao Jaan came only in 1986. Hariprasad had notched up a fair number of memorable films much before that.

Among them, one that stands out in both his own and public memory, for the role the flute played in the music and in the film itself, is *Hero*.

An Interlude

The surroundings are rocky and picturesque. The hero, dressed in a colourful T-shirt that has seen better days, with a red band wrapped around his head, wears his hobo look with much ease. But the sound of his flute is clear and enchanting. The tune floats out across the stony wastes, through the closed doors of a makeshift bamboo shelter, and awakens the beauty sleeping within. Hearing the sound of the flute, she runs out, and quite forgetting herself, dances and hums along.

The tune is indeed catchy. It plays repeatedly in the film, a leitmotif that takes the story forward at each point it is played.

To begin with, Bharat Bhushan plays it. He is a street player at that moment in the film, whatever else he might have been earlier in the story. His wife lies in the throes of impending death, but unaware of it, he plays, hoping to garner enough money for her treatment. Their son, wide-eyed, wonders why his father does not go up to collect the notes from the leering shopkeeper who is offering money in denominations of 100.

The poignancy of the scene is reason enough for the tune to remain emblazoned in the boy's memory, and for him to play it at every turning point in his life.

On Independence Day, he plays it in the jail where he has been incarcerated for two years, thus earning brownie points; he plays it at sad moments and triumphant ones.

By the time the film is over, the tune has imprinted itself in the audience's mind.

Till date, it continues to be one of the most memorable tunes with the highest recall. And is still available as a ringtone, forty years after the movie's release.

Subhash Ghai, who produced and directed *Hero*, has never forgotten the story behind the tune that has remained the most popular of the compositions in his many blockbuster films, including *Karz, Taal, Saudagar* and *Ram Lakhan.*

'Every instrument has its language,' he says. 'The guitar is a young instrument, the electric guitar has violent energy, it shouts. It suits a kind of film theme. In *Kalicharan*, for example, I used brass, there were fights, victory . . . they needed loud, clanging sounds. And of course, the guitar was paramount in *Karz*. But when I was making *Hero*, I was looking for a different kind of music. Something traditional.

'The shehnai is traditional, but it has a strong pull on emotions; it pulls them out from even the most practical mind. The flute, on the other hand, is softer, more romantic. The flute is a part of our cultural heritage, Kishen played it. In fact, when I was planning Whistling Woods, I imagined a man standing on top of a mountain listening to the wind whistling through the woods. He plucks a bamboo, makes holes in it and begins to play, and the flute is created. There is divine power in the instrument; played only with six fingers and breath, it creates notes, songs, ragas, through wind. The thought impressed me. I named the school Whistling Woods.

'I had been impressed by the music of two films, *Baiju Bawra*, *Phagun*. When I became a filmmaker, I realized the flute was used in romantic interludes; it was soothing, the prime choice for bhakti or sringar ras. Any scene of crying, bonding, separation, and the flute would be there in the background.

'I had written *Hero* as a Radha–Kishen story. The heroine was called Radha, the hero Jaikishen, so he could be Jackie. Automatically, the flute was my choice for the film. I include the music when I write a film, discuss [it] with the composer when engaging him. The theme was clear. Radha and Kishen. He happens to be a gangster, but the son of a flute player, who breathes through the flute, is passionate about the instrument. When the father dies playing the flute, the son picks it up, picks up his father's tune and continues to play it whenever he is emotional.

'Laxmikant–Pyarelal were my music directors for the film. I explained to them the importance of the flute, told them the story; they loved it. I had always been a fan of the flute. In the '50s, I was a big fan of Pannalal Ghosh; would listen to him on the radio. Then I heard Hari-ji. He creates a relationship with the audience in a personal way. His flute lingers on after the show is over, like classic movies linger on.

'My relationship with Hariprasad started with CDs, as a listener. I never thought then, I would share the stage with him. I had first seen him during the background score of *Krodhi*. He closes his eyes when he plays, and shuts the world out. I noticed that. It impressed me.

'I told Pyare-ji during the music discussions of *Hero*, when LP had just recorded the first piece, "I want a strong instrumental piece, like in *Karz*." Both of them unanimously decided on Chaurasia.

'He was a VIP instrumentalist, [the] highest paid musician then, even if he was only playing in the background. Yet, when I met him, he was humble . . . though I knew he had great pride in his talent and music.

'I remember, Pyarelal played three options he had composed on the piano. Hari-ji had not yet come then. When he came, he took notes from Pyarelal and said, "Give me ten minutes, I will compose." He noticed, too, that I was discussing with Pyare. I had become known for my ear, after *Karz*.

'He prepared the tune, we okayed it. The take was on. I went to him and said, "I want to narrate the story." He was taken aback. I told him, "*Meri film ki atma aapke haathon mein hain* . . . the soul of my film is in your hands. You and I both like the notes you have created, but how will you play the tune?" I then narrated the story of Bharat Bhushan and his son. He listened. Then his face lit up. Brightened. He said, "Give me twenty minutes." After twenty minutes, he called me back in. He pointed to his box, *peti*, and opened his wooden box. I think there were fifty flutes inside . . . thin, small, big, fat . . . And he said, "Which would you like me to play?" I replied, "I want a high note, something that will resound into valleys of love." So he picked a few, and played three or four. I said, "This one." He nodded.

'He retreated into a corner, then, after playing alone, as if in dhyan, he came back and asked, "Can I play the same notes with this?" He played the notes so peacefully, after taking approval from Pyarelal. At the recording, he played the same notes so well, it was magical. I knew in that moment that my picture would be a hit.

'The tune inspired A.R. Rahman to accept *Taal*. He played the flute tune on his keyboard on stage. In my film *Krishna* too, Hariprasad Chaurasia was the obvious choice. There is no flute player close to him in genius.'

Ghai also underlines the popularity of Hariprasad's composition for *Hero* when he recounts the story the flautist told his audience at a function at Ghai's Whistling Woods multi-discipline educational complex in north Bombay.

'He had come for a culture workshop. He told us, "Wherever I go for classical programmes, I eventually also have to play the *Hero* tune, because people start shouting. There is something in that tune . . . I have played so many things, but people remember that tune. So even though I don't want to, I end up playing it." That is an indirect compliment to me, and a tribute from audiences to his own genius.'

It is now his practice to enter the studio only when all the initial rehearsals are done, and the composer is ready for a take. 'Often the scriptwriter, cameraman, director, singers, all would be ready. I would rush in at the last moment. Everyone knew I would add my notes in as I thought fit, and it would be correct.'

But not everyone was given the right to make last-minute interventions. Hariprasad was often witness to differences of opinion between music directors and producers, with each holding his own ground.

He remembers one such incident between music director Roshan and Sheikh Mukhtar.

'Roshan sahab was a small-made man, but with big talent. And sometimes could show temper. It had been a long day, a song had just been recorded, and the clock showed 11 p.m. Mukhtar said he wanted to change a line or the full song, I forget which. Roshan got very angry. He refused, but Mukhtar insisted. Finally Roshan threw up his hands and said, "You compose it yourself." A huge argument followed, with everyone shouting. Meanwhile, the meter was ticking ticking, money was going, going.

'Mukhtar said, "It is my money, I am paying for the film, so I want the change." Roshan said, "Why couldn't you tell me earlier . . . why now, so late . . ." Mukhtar said, "Well, ideas can come anytime."

'Luckily for all of us, it got solved,' he adds, laughing at the memory.

Hariprasad's memories include a snapshot of O.P. Nayyar. Whimsical and headstrong, the rhythm king would hand out 100-rupee notes from his pocket if he was happy with his recording. 'If I was late for his recording, he would gesture to me from the studio window to play. And once I was done, would pull out 100 rupees from his pocket and press it into my hand. Other times, he has been known to hand 100-rupee notes to beggars as he walked by the seaside.'

Hariprasad is now everybody's friend, favourite of many music directors. 'Like me, music director Ravi-ji loved cars. Those days, he had an Impala which he loved driving around. After a session at the studio, he would say, "I will drop you." Sometimes, if a recording got cancelled, he would whisk me off to his favourite mithai shop and we would stuff ourselves with jalebis and other sweets, after which we would happily get into the car, and he would drop me back.'

Recording sessions were a whole different ball game back then, Hariprasad reminisces, adding that the singer and the entire orchestra would first rehearse thoroughly, and then the take would begin. 'A single mistake, an instrument playing at the wrong time or playing out of tune, and the entire take would have to be redone. It was a matter of perfect mutual coordination and understanding. And unless it was a music director like Naushad, whom even K. Asif sahab could not persuade to change anything, music sessions were collaborative activities. I remember, in one scene, actor Dharmendra suggested the music interlude be extended, because he was shown on screen as running down the steps. 'It needs more time, I need more time,' he said. His suggestion was accepted.

'Sometimes, after getting the tune from the music director, I would start to play, and an assistant might suggest I try an alaap here, or suggest the director add a rhythm to the dance there . . . ideas were freely welcomed and exchanged. I have even seen the director dance to show how Bhagwan should move.'

Little wonder the hours slipped past, and Hariprasad was seldom seen at home. He loved his work, but also knew that his wife was alone, fretting at home. He laughs as he remembers an occasion when he was at the studio with Raj Kapoor who was working with Shankar–Jaikishen on a song. 'The recording was on, RK was listening, the glass he was sipping from was in one corner. Jaikishen too held a drink. They would sip and listen, then a new idea would come up. Time and again, the recording would be stopped, as ideas bounced about. I was worried. At 1 a.m., I finally said, "*Mera divorce ho jayega!*" I will face a divorce! Raj-ji said, "*Number deejiye,*" and picking up the receiver, he called my house. Anuradha picked up the phone. He said, "Raj Kapoor speaking." Anuradha was surprised, excited. Then he said, "I am holding your husband back at the studio for a while longer." That night, Anuradha did not seem to mind my coming in only early in the morning.'

Often, Hariprasad would accompany the showman and others to his bungalow in Loni, 'a time of happy creative memories'.

An Interlude

Anuradha is surprised when the doorbell rings. It is close to midnight, and she is alone at home, as Hariprasad is still at some recording. She hastens to the door. The grille is shut, but two men stand outside. One of them is a sardar. She can smell liquor, and is filled with unease.

'Bhabhi-ji, we came to give you this, it is my first recording.'

'I realized it was Jagjit Singh, and relaxed,' she says, laughing.

'The songs were *"Apna gham bhool gaye"* and one other number . . . I played it on the radiogram we had those days. When Manorama heard it, she fell in love with the voice. "What a wonderful voice!" she kept saying.'

Jagjit Singh would later become one of the Chaurasia couple's closest friends.

On 5 October 2018, Pt Hariprasad Chaurasia and Pt Shivkumar Sharma are participating in a programme called '*Baaton Baaton Mein*' organized by Banyan Tree under its Kala Virasat section. The two friends sit under a spotlight on the vast stage of the Nehru Centre in Bombay, and are to share with the public stories from their five-decade-long musical journey together.

What follows is unlike anything the public were expecting. No long-winded telling of ups and downs, no well-repeated anecdotes. Perfect foils to each other, Shivkumar sits bolt upright, as if ready to play the santoor, while Hariprasad sits back comfortably in his chair, looking like a happy Buddha as he parries with his old-time friend.

'I first noticed Shiv-ji in Bombay, when I was still new to the city,' he recounts. 'We were at a studio, at the same time. We met by chance. I had not seen anything beautiful in this busy, mechanical city. When I saw this man, he looked beautiful, so I kept looking till 2 in the morning. Till the recording finished.' The flautist grins mischievously when he notices his friend's obvious embarrassment.

Shivkumar's first impressions are of a man immersed in his music. 'His riyaz was no less than the *chaar-mombati* (four-candle) riyaz that would go on till the candles burnt down one by one. In the studio, I would notice how, even as all the musicians and the singer would move into the other room, while the soundtrack was being recorded and they waited to be called up again, he would sit back by himself and practise fingering on the flute. Technique is not everything; music must touch the soul. That does not come from riyaz, his playing is a blessing from God. It touches the soul of the listener, whether it is a layman or expert. It also comes from his persona.'

Hariprasad responds with, 'I learnt a lot watching how intently and creatively Shivkumar played his santoor.'

The duo narrate stories of their days as performing artistes with ITC's Sangeet Research Academy (SRA), set up by the corporate group to foster a gurukul-like teaching system. Besides finding and training talent under the tutelage of well-known maestros, SRA took musicians on tours to bring the richness of India's musical heritage to small-towners as well. Pt Vijay Kichlu, a reputed gharane-dar musician, was entrusted with the task of turning the idea of the SRA into reality.

'It was a period of learning for us too,' Hariprasad says. 'We would tour the villages by bus, interact with the villagers, and perform. It was one way of knowing the country closely. But there is one trip I will never forget,' he adds, looking at his friend, and the two laugh at the memory evoked.

'We were in some small town and the bus driver took a few wrong turns and lost his way. There was no one to ask directions, it was dark, and the place was quite deserted. We told the driver, keep driving, we will reach somewhere. Finally, in front of us, we saw a bullock cart. And luckily, there was a man in it. Someone, I think it was Kichlu, who felt responsible for us, jumped out and asked the cart man for directions. The man said, "You are not far away from the main road, I can show you." He flicked his whip and the bullocks moved, the creaking cart wheels rolled slowly ahead. And on that narrow road, twisting and turning through many small lanes, the bus full of musicians drove painfully in first gear, for an hour or more, till he finally pointed to a branching road and told us to drive that way.'

The deadpan voice in which the story is narrated brings the house down, as does the picture his words paint of a bus solemnly following a bullock cart on a dark village road.

The two friends knit their lives around music. More often than not, they are part of the same orchestra at recordings. And each in his own way is making it obvious to music directors and arrangers that they can add in the suitable bits themselves, and do not need to read off a readymade music score sheet.

Among their favourites is the title song of the Asha Parekh–Dharmendra starrer *Aaye Din Bahar Ke*, which released in 1966. The song is a celebration of spring, and even as Lata Mangeshkar's voice rises in an unforgettable alaap, and goes on to the mukhda calling her lover to her, the camera tilts up to show trees in full bloom, misty hills in the distance and flowers lining the heroine's pathway. 'The arranger would give the song's notation to instrumentalists and explain the situation, and tell us to play,' Shivkumar explains.

Once the mukhda of the song is over, the santoor begins the interlude, gently dancing on heartstrings, and the flute starts warbling almost immediately, as the heroine runs down innumerable steps on seeing the hero wending his way up the mountain path. The flute and santoor are again evident in the interlude before the second antara, but in keeping with the visual, are softer, more romantic, and the sitar comes in. Little wonder then that music directors Laxmikant–Pyarelal gave the duo a free hand. In fact, Hariprasad would go on to be a veritable constant at their recordings, and be given a carte blanche to add in the flute as and when he thought it fitting.

The year 1966 is noteworthy for another evocative film with a great musical score, *Milan*. Hariprasad teaches Sunil Dutt, the hero, to hold the flute and blow into it convincingly, much as he will teach Rajendra Kumar four years later, when the star plays a flute-playing villager in *Geet*. Marking a first in the history of film credits, Hariprasad's name will feature as the flautist whose flute plays all through the film, through the hero's persona.

A year after *Aaye Din Bahar Ke*, in 1967, *Hamraaz* would be released by B.R. Chopra. The duo were part of music director Ravi's ensemble of instrumentalists, although, individually, each enjoyed a different status.

It is around the time of the making of *Hamraaz* that the next milestone in Hariprasad's life is set.

'By now, we were a musical duo. Though opposites in nature, there were so many common interests between us. We loved the same foods; in fact, we just loved food and thought nothing of driving two or three hours to a restaurant for a good meal. We loved to travel, and enjoyed long drives. And our wives got on wonderfully together,' Shivkumar says, counting on his fingers the many points where the two concurred. 'Then of course, above all, there was the music and our own dreams of getting our instruments recognized in their own right as worthy of playing solo in classical music.

'During *Hamraaz*, when the recording of scores for fight sequences were on, we would sit and chat with Yash Chopra. We found much common ground. Yash-ji was very musical. When he started his own films, he would call to ask when we were free to come in. Khayyam was directing the music for *Kabhi Kabhie*. Yash-ji would know where he wanted the flute or santoor. When the background music was being discussed, he would include us in the situation. When the recording was on, he realized we were composing our own pieces.'

Hariprasad also remembers that epic moment when the iconic director literally handed the baton to them. 'Yash-ji would watch while the orchestra was recording, and see who was contributing in what way. He realized we could play even without a music director instructing or guiding us. When the music director said, "Do as you please", we would offer a piece that was a perfect fit. So, he said to us, "Why do you not make music?" . . . And the offer followed.'

Yash Chopra, whose films are landmarks of romance and great music, was in many ways a trailblazer. His choice of locations in Switzerland has been a boost to its gains in tourism from India with special 'film location' tours as part of the itineraries on offer. Quick to see an opportunity to pave a new path, Chopra told the two musicians, 'I want you to create music for my next film.' The 'next film' to be made under the Yash Chopra banner would be *Silsila*. Much would have changed in the musicians' lives by the time the film was launched, in 1980. As Shivkumar puts it simply, 'By that time, we were known the world over as classical musicians.'

The years between 1966 and 1975 are a period when Hariprasad's life takes sharp turns. The ups and downs are like a rollercoaster ride, and life moves so quickly that he has little time to take note of his surroundings as he is carried along by the flow of destiny. For one, his entire attitude to the flute has changed. He has brought down the walls that the reclusive wife of Pt Ravi Shankar, sitar maestro, had built around herself, and has persuaded her to teach him classical music. He has put away the short bamboo flutes he has played till then and taken up the longer instrument, which demands more from its players by way of breath and finger movement. But even as he spends hours at his new, hard-won guru's feet, he continues to play for films. And adds international tours to his calendar.

He remembers the high of playing solo at Royal Albert Hall in London. The applause of the appreciative audience often rings in his ears. He hopes to hear the applause again. He knows too, he will find a way to take his flute and his music to audiences far beyond his own homeland.

The big break comes sooner than Chopra's 'next film'. Already the signs are obvious.

In 1967, Laxmikant–Pyarelal win a special award for *Milan* given by St Xavier's College, Bombay. Mukesh and Anand Bakshi are also honoured, as is Hariprasad for his contribution as flautist. Indeed, rightfully so, as the songs lean heavily on the flute in the film. The duo win the Filmfare Award for best musical direction too, though Mukesh loses out to Mahendra Kapoor in *Hamraaz*.

The only link between the winning song in *Hamraaz*, 'Nile gagan ke tale', and the songs in *Milan*, is that in both, Hariprasad's flute has a starring role.

This is also the year that the quiet friendship between two dedicated musicians becomes a public collaborative enterprise.

'We planned in our discussions to find a way to play together, it was our constant dream.'

'We were meeting every day, something had to come out of it that was musically new.'

Though these two sentences spoken by Hariprasad and Shivkumar use different words, they do say much the same thing, echoing their need to create something that would showcase the depth of their mastery and knowledge of their instruments and music. Approaching HMV, they put forth a plan for a new composition of songs that could be recorded as an offering by them. U.K. Dubey who held the power to say yes or no fights shy of the idea, saying the risk is too big, the company runs on Lata Mangeshkar's name.

However, all is not lost. Hariprasad smilingly recollects, 'J.N. Joshi, a singer and musician himself, offered to put up the idea at the next internal meeting at HMV. He suggested the music should be thematic, classical with a lot of instrumentation, adding vocals only if required. He thought of a mood of "yog", near the Ganga. We set to work. It was very exciting, but also a huge challenge.'

'We recruited Pt Brijbhushan Kabra who played the slide guitar,' Shivkumar remembers. 'He was in the same boat as us, no one had ever heard the slide guitar played in classical music, but he was a master of his craft. Manikrao Popatkar provided the tabla support.'

The trio meet every day, discussions and music sessions follow, each bringing in what could work, and the others examining, accepting and integrating. 'Soon, we composed eight or nine pieces,' Hariprasad says.

Shivkumar already had an EP (Extended Play 45 rpm vinyl record) released by HMV. Besides, the santoor had figured prominently in the *Jhanak Jhanak* movie score. Hariprasad had also ensured the presence of the flute in film music across languages. The trio were sanguine about their compositions being kindly received by HMV.

'Dubey said, "Try something different in this presentation. Try to knit it into a theme." I told him nothing like this has been done, but we decided to give it a thought,' Shivkumar recalls how they created songs in line with Dubey's advice.

'I thought of a day in the life of a shepherd in the Kashmir valley. I made a story around it. And we composed along the storyline. The songs were recorded. Joshi wrote a poetic composition around the songs, and it was carried along with the details of the ragas, on the back of the LP.'

In his autobiography *Journey with a Hundred Strings: My Life in Music*, co-authored by Ira Puri, Shivkumar Sharma speaks at length on how the valley of Kashmir inspired his compositions. 'I thought of the breeze rippling through the grass, flocks of sheep grazing, and the splashing brook glinting in the rays of the sun. Finally, I saw myself representing the experience on my santoor strings, trying to capture my enchanting environs in my music . . . J.N. Joshi agreed to pen the sleeve notes, a sort of screenplay describing each section . . . the finale was the shepherd meeting his beloved in the shikara, and I admit I put all my heart into composing that scene.'

The record, *Call of the Valley*, grabbed the imagination of the public, exceeding the expectations of the artistes who created the music as well as those of the company that produced the vinyl. Hariprasad believes the story made the music easier to understand, even for the lay person, adding a romantic aura. Soon, extra copies had to be created to meet the growing demand. Quick to see potential, HMV commissioned a follow-up a few years later, but *The Valley Recalls* would not match the success of the first record.

Finally, as Hariprasad puts it simply, 'HMV got tired of making editions of *Call of the Valley* and sold the master copy to an English company, who is still selling it. But it made our instruments known to the world.'

One measure of the popularity of *Call of the Valley* is that it has featured in the list of *1001 Albums You Must Hear Before You Die*, a musical reference book launched in 2005 by Universe Publishing, as well as a listing by the *Guardian*, UK, of '50 Essential CDs from Around the World'.

Laughing about the trend that the success of *Call of the Valley* evoked, Hariprasad lists the many that followed. '*Call of the Mountains, Song of the Rivers, Music of the Rivers* . . . luckily no one thought of a collection called Call of Nature.'

Six simple, melodious, classical music-based tunes form the text of Shiv–Hari's bestselling offering to the public. The raga story starting with Ahir Bhairav delineates the early hours of the morning, when, 'twinkling stars are trailing behind a pale moon in the West, while the horizon in the East gradually assumes a crimson hue, heralding the approach of dawn. The tiny hamlet, nestling amidst the snow-capped peaks gradually comes out of slumber.' The note goes on to explain that the slow notes of the guitar portray the advent of dawn. The twinkling notes of the santoor come dancing on the first rays of the sun and join the notes of the guitar. The play together of the two instruments depicts the heightening tempo as the hour advances. All these are tunefully woven . . . in Raga Ahir Bhairav . . . a morning raga.

The note goes on to explain in a few sentences the significance of the raga and its position as a morning raga in the lexicon of Hindustani classical music.

In the second movement, the music flows into another morning raga, Nat Bhairav, which according to Joshi's explanation, enlarges the image of the beautiful valley where bees buzz and lovebirds jump from one branch to another, even as dawn gives way to daylight.

The sheep come in to graze. The stage is set for the hero's entry, with the guitar, flute and santoor combining to create anticipation with their music. By the time the tabla has worked up to a crescendo, the hero has arrived on the scene, and, drunk with the beauty of his surroundings, sits in a trance-like state under a tree to await the arrival of his beloved.

The composition now moves to the melodic Raga Piloo, where guitar and santoor usher in the girl, tremulous, yet happy. The music symbolizes the meeting—the lover teasing, mock-angry at the late arrival of the beloved, and the dialogue that follows. Drama ensues as the flute breaks in, to tell the lovers there are intruding eyes watching their tryst. The girl runs away, the boy asking her to wait, but getting only a promise of a meeting later that evening. Again, the rhythm of the tabla heightens the tension, leaving the audience in suspense, as Side One of the LP comes to an end.

The first composition on Side Two of the LP does nothing to ease the tension. Instead, the instruments combine in slow dhrupad style to create a devotional mood in Raga Bhoop. The flute is joined by the santoor and the guitar in a slow composition that tugs at the listener's heartstrings. The music continues as the hero joins the devout in the gathering dusk, as the temple bells call for prayer, to pray for a meeting with his lady love. Using the pakhavaj, a booming, older instrument that predates the tabla, the rhythm is heavy, in a ten-beat jhap taal cycle.

Melody rules the next movement, in Raga Desh, wherein, 'a leisurely alaap of the flute serves as a beacon' to the lovers. The scene Joshi creates is idyllic, with the moon rising, the snow-topped mountains glistening in the moonlight, and the lovers wending their way to their secret tryst. Flute and santoor play a heady background song that heightens the romance of the mood as they meet and, unafraid now of prying eyes, walk together. The evening composition ends with the discovery of a hidden lake with a boat floating on it.

Perhaps it is the final movement in the love story and the composition that closes it that accounts for the thundering success of the LP. Set in Raga Pahadi, with distinct Kashmiri overtones, the celebratory music sees the lovers gliding away in the boat into a space from which they never wish to return. Flute and santoor set the mood; then the flute lets the santoor sing while the guitar creates a lilting background that mimics the rise and fall of oars as the boat glides away. The instruments marry in perfect harmony and the listener is left with a feeling of inner joy, after his senses have wandered amidst the beautiful sights of the Valley along with the now-happy lovers.

The cover design by Amar Paul, showing pines and a meadow against snow-clad mountains and our shepherd with his flock around him meeting his beloved by the side of a lake whose waters reflect their images, lent visual appeal to an intensely felt musical creation, giving it a touch of universal magic.

Little wonder that *Call of the Valley* remains the bestselling of Indian classical instrumental compositions, till date, according to the *Guardian*, UK.

An Interlude

'Once Nargis approached music director S.D. Burman. She wanted him to sing for an event being organized by the association she spearheaded. "Sing any folk song," she told the director, when he demurred. He said, "I don't sing," but she would not take no for an answer, and got him to agree.

'He came to me and Avni Dasgupta. "You will play for me," he said. "We will meet at six that evening," he added, which was early for a programme that was to start at eight.

'I reached the venue, Rang Bhawan, at 6 p.m. Burman dada was already at the venue, sitting at the back, in white dhoti and kurta. The watchman had already told me as I entered, that there was no one . . . only Burman dada, alone.

'I sat down next to him; he was sweating nervously. He held my hand and said, "Good you came, I was dying . . ."

'He would keep asking every few minutes, "*Baby aya kya?*" Has Baby (meaning Nargis) come? I told him she would come by 7.30. He kept telling me to call her. "Tell her I am not well, drop the idea."

'Then he looked searchingly at me, so I asked, "What is it?" He said, "Can I get a drop?" I replied, "We are near Metro, I live in Bandra, how do I know where to get anything here." "*Main mar jaoonga, aap mujhe maar jaate ho.*"

'Finally, a driver went and managed to get some liquor from some Christian shop. He drank it all in one gulp. Then asked, "Where is the stage?"

'Meanwhile, the audience had started taking its seats. Burman dada said, "I am going now." I told him, "Not yet, only when audience is settled." He said ok, then started singing loudly backstage. I asked him what he was singing. He said, "Arey bhai, *aaj chandni raat* (today is a moonlit night), you show them the moon." He kept singing for ten minutes. Then got up and left quickly in his Fiat. I left too.

'But Nargis was happy. She had created history by making him sing at a private function.'

The same year, Hariprasad realized another dream—to work closely with Lata Mangeshkar.

Any artiste growing up far away from the city that spins dreams through the medium of cinema harbours a desire to work with the industry titans. Actors hope to work under the baton of great directors who will make them immortal through their films, while singers and musicians dream of working with leading singers and music directors. As Jagjit Singh would dream of creating an album with Lata Mangeshkar, many years later, Hariprasad too hopes to get to know the singer closer on musical terms. They have interacted at recordings; he knows she looks upon him with smiling, kind eyes. But he wishes for more.

The opportunity presents itself soon enough. His prodigious talent has not gone unnoticed. Soon, he is playing happily on his flute for the Nightingale's private recordings set to music by her brother, Hridaynath Mangeshkar, which include the iconic *Gyaneshwari* album and '*Mogra Phulala*'.

'They must be fifty-sixty in number,' Hariprasad lists, 'from the Geeta, Upanishads onwards, I played for all her private songs, which we recorded at the HMV studio.' To borrow a line from

S.D. Burman when recounting a well-known story about Hariprasad and a tin of rosogullas, from the book *Sun Mere Bandhu Re: The Musical Journey of S.D. Burman*, 'Lata always said, Hari plays very sweetly.'

By the 1970s, the world of music was changing, merging. India was beckoning the West, as strongly as the West had beckoned India.

Hariprasad talks about the late 1960s, when the Beatles were looking for new pastures.

India was not new to the four members of the rock band which had won worldwide popularity not just for their music but also because they were a symbol of rebellious youth with their mop-like haircuts and their free use of psychedelic drugs such as LSD. But, in 1967, George Harrison, the band's lead guitarist had discovered the magnetism of Maharishi Mahesh Yogi and his mantra of Transcendental Meditation, popularly abbreviated to TM.

The Beatles had fallen under the Maharishi's spell in 1967, when they attended a seminar conducted by him in Wales. Plans to join him at his ashram in Rishikesh were temporarily shelved due to unforeseen circumstances, including the death of Brian Epstein, their manager. But not long after, the Beatles would start making trips to India, curious about the culture and people of the country. Naturally, though, these were necessarily surreptitious visits.

'Of course, knowing their huge fan following across the world, they travelled in disguise,' Hariprasad explains. 'They had become Krishna bhakts, and loved the sound of the flute. They would come home, lounge around listening to music, have their drugs.' While the flautist was not really aware of the band's popularity, sitar maestro Ravi Shankar knew.

Though there were no plans at that time, this early interaction would lead to future collaborations in which Hariprasad would play a vital role.

The Beatles were to come back to India in February 1968.

Harrison, who was working on the soundtrack of the film *Wonderwall*, came a month earlier to record the portions that needed Indian instruments. He would include the santoor by Shivkumar Sharma along with the sarod, tar sarod and shehnai in his composition.

Making the most of the opportunity, Harrison would also record the instrumental track of a lesser known single, '*The Inner Light*', the only Beatle studio recording done outside Europe. '*The Inner Light*' would use the pakhavaj, the sarod, the shehnai, and the flute played by Hariprasad Chaurasia.

In February 1968, the press was agog with news of the Beatles visiting Rishikesh. This time they came openly, with a huge retinue made up of girlfriends, wives, assistants, along with the international press trailing after them. By this time, the group was speaking publicly about the power TM gave them as creative performers as compared to what they had derived from taking drugs.

But the trip to Rishikesh, though fruitful in terms of the songs that emerged out of the visit and from the interactions with the Maharishi as well as other celebrity Western performers who were present there, would hold a mirror to the slowly disintegrating relationships in the world's most-loved band of that time. Reports of their guru's alleged misbehaviour with women devotees made George Harrison, his chief follower from the group, leave Rishikesh to go back home within two months, with John Lennon accompanying him. Ringo Starr and

Paul McCartney had already left earlier, each for his own personal reasons.

All that would remain of the TM experience would be a tourist spot that still draws the curious tourist in Rishikesh to the 'ashram where the Beatles lived' and Harrison's continued involvement with India, which, though centred on Ravi Shankar, his sitar guru, would involve Hariprasad too.

Meanwhile, there are other developments in the flautist's life.

Anuradha and Hariprasad welcome their son, Rajeev, into their lives in October 1968. The child brings new joys to both parents, and also alleviates his mother's feeling of being alone at home, thanks to her husband's continued involvement with his music.

Two years later, in 1971, on a tour of Europe, Hariprasad and Shivkumar record a *jugalbandi* album for a Swedish company. Playing two classical ragas, the instrumentalists demonstrate the universal quality of their instruments. When the company realizes the two names are too long to fit into the cover, they hit upon the term Shiv–Hari as an alternative. 'I am January-born, he is born in July, so I am only six months older, but he treats me like an elder brother,' Shivkumar says, by way of explanation for why his friend insisted Shiv should precede Hari in the double-barrelled name. But by all counts, it was a lucky thought. The name stuck, and would be seen on film posters soon enough.

The year 1974 will see other milestones in Hariprasad's life. He is by now a much-invited performer across European countries. He continues to create background scores for Oriya films as part of the Bhuban–Hari team of composers. And his flute is heard across films in all languages.

No surprise then, when an impassioned young man, freshly back from the US where he has been to study filmmaking, decides to make a breakaway film that runs against the grain of Hollywood blockbusters, and turns to Bhuban–Hari. Perhaps, his reasons were the same as another filmmaker who turned to a classical artiste, Ravi Shankar, for his first film, *Pather Panchali* (1955), hoping for music different from the familiar tunes from established directors, whom he cannot afford anyway.

In fact, for his debut feature film, *27 Down*, the director, Awtar Kaul, has picked a cast that is more known for its acting prowess than star power, with Rakhee Gulzar, an already established heroine, as the only possible exception. The film has M.K. Raina, Sadhu Meher, Om Shivpuri and Rekha Sabnis as part of the cast to bring alive on celluloid Ramesh Bakshi's Hindi novel *Athara Sooraj ke Paudhe*.

Hariprasad talks about the assignment of composing for Kaul's film.

'I hesitated a bit. But I had already started composing in 1965, when I recorded a series of cassettes at home. I happened to hear a German boy playing tunes on the keyboard. He was composing his own music. I liked his music. So I invited him, and we decided to create some recordings. He would play his tunes, I would add to it on my flute, and every night, after dinner, I would rest for a bit for one to two hours, then we would record till 4 a.m., after which I would sleep, so I could be fresh for work in the morning. The cassettes had names like *Now, Here, Out of the Blues* and *Meditative Romance*. He would take copies of the cassette and leave it with a distributor, and collect the money from sales every evening, minus the distributor's commission. But this was different. Kaul was asking me to create music for a film, both offbeat and sombre in tone. I thought about it, but decided to go ahead.'

Hariprasad rises to the occasion. The film's credits include Bhuban–Hari as music directors. Surjit Singh adds that the flautist recruited other classical instrumentalists, including Zakir Hussain, Zarine Daruwalla, and the sarangi maestro Pt Ram Narayan, to create a score befitting a film that challenged the tried-and-tested norms in Hindi films, in every way.

In *27 Down*, the sounds of everyday life play a major role. The rat-a-tat of the train on the tracks, the sound of a ball being bounced, the hiss of the engine as it sends out steam—these are almost the only sounds one hears in the early scenes of the film. Kaul uses silence too very effectively, and it is to the music directors' credit that they do not give in to the temptation to intervene.

The background music is first heard when the film is almost ten minutes underway. The sarod with a faraway flute create a gentle backdrop to the scene. A few minutes later, as the young hero explores the environs of the railway station, wandering about the yard, walking on a single rail, the flute is joyous and the sarod sings merrily along. The same restraint is evident in the school master's song, '*Chuk chuk*

chuk chuk chalti rail, which recreates the rhythm of the train through strings, and later the clapping of hands while the flute stands in for the whistle. The film is thus treated in a way that the music never overshadows a mood or a scene, but tends to underline it gently, leading the viewer deeper into the desired emotion.

The score Bhuban–Hari create for *27 Down* does not go unnoticed. Though they were mostly creating background music in Oriya films till then, the duo are now invited to also direct the songs. In 1975, they would compose for *Samaya*, which would include Manna Dey delivering a hit song, and a year later, *Gapa Hele bi Sata*, Orissa's first full-colour movie, which had songs by Suman Kalyanpur and Amit Kumar among others. *Ma o Mamta* would follow by 1980.

And in 1980, Yash Chopra would make *Silsila*.

Classical Yearnings: The Artiste as Student

The music of *Silsila* owes as much to the collaborative genius of Shiv–Hari as it does to the intense training Hariprasad was receiving in classical music and flute-playing techniques from his new guru, Annapurna Devi.

In a rare book titled *An Unheard Melody: Annapurna Devi, An Authorized Biography*, Swapan Kumar Bandyopadhyay, her devoted student, unspools the reasons why the gifted daughter of Ustad Allauddin Khan who had fallen in love with and married her father's student, sitar player Ravi Shankar, moved away from life with him and practised her art as almost a complete recluse. Quoting Annapurna Devi, the book says, 'My first performance was a duet in Delhi. I remember Pandit-ji telling me before the performance that I should cater a little to the public taste. My response was that I would play only what I was taught. I think the audience enjoyed my playing . . . Whenever I performed, people appreciated my playing, and I sensed that Pandit-ji was not too happy with the response. I was not that fond of performing anyway, so I stopped it and continued my sadhana.'

Later in the chapter, Bandyopadhyay goes on to say that when Annapurna Devi accompanied her husband to perform at about five public concerts to raise money to alleviate his debt, comparisons were often heard being made. 'It was reportedly said that in her music there was 80 per cent Baba Allauddin Khan, while Ali Akbar had 70 per cent and Ravi Shankar had 40 per cent.' Such remarks would further alienate the sitarist from his wife.

Hrishikesh Mukherjee, in his sensitively made film *Abhimaan*, reportedly mined this unspoken rivalry of the husband towards his more talented wife. Though at the time of its release, the general public thought that the Amitabh Bachchan–Jaya Bhaduri starrer was actually fashioned on their own relationship, the real inspiration possibly lay deeper in the past.

In *Abhimaan*, the couple are both singers, and the husband finds himself being overshadowed by his wife, who not only has a natural gift but has been taught by her father, a singer himself. A rift develops and the two are estranged. Luckily for the audience, whose sympathies lie with the heroine who has not wilfully tried to shine above her husband, the hero comes to his senses and the marriage is saved. The film ends with them singing on stage together.

Annapurna's marriage would, however, crack beyond repair. Reporting on an argument which raged between Ravi Shankar and his wife, Bandyopadhyay concludes by writing, 'The jugalbandis, in their five or six concerts together, were enough to establish her superiority over Ravi Shankar as a performer and a musician. That time, Ravi did not know she would willingly withdraw herself from the public eye. She was on the rise. The connoisseurs hailed her as great. The surbahar also helped establish her supremacy, because it is a more difficult instrument than the sitar, heavier and more satisfying musically.'

The text goes on to explain, 'Ravi was justifiably jealous. And so he elicited a vow from his wife that she would no longer play in public. There are many versions of this anecdote afloat, mostly apocryphal. Annapurna herself told me something much worse had happened than Ravi attempting to make her take this oath. But she added she would divulge it to no one. "This will go with me when I go," she said emphatically.'

When Hariprasad decides to seek out Annapurna Devi, many friends warn him he is like a child crying for the moon. Annapurna lives alone, shut up in her flat, and will not open the door to visitors. And no, she was not inclined to take students beyond the few she had already agreed to teach.

The reasons for Hariprasad seeking a guru are manifold. For one, 'I was doing very well, but I was missing my classical music. There was no time for it. And I felt I was losing my touch, getting mechanical in my playing. More often than not, my interventions in the music were for ten to thirty seconds, except in rare cases. How could I grow as an artiste with that! I realized the only way to progress to where I wanted my music to go was to find a guru and immerse myself in learning.'

In the NCPA face-to-face interview, he cites another reason. 'Sanjeev Kumar, the actor, once told me, "I see you as Hariprasad Chaurasia, the flautist, not as a music director sitting with a harmonium." The comment shocked me at first, but also touched my heart. I thought I should leave films. Why was I slogging for banks to enjoy my money?'

At home, too, he was often gently steered towards his first love, classical music. 'Learn classical music, find a teacher!' Anuradha would coax, seeing her husband running day and night between studios. She felt he was losing touch with his classical roots. 'I could not exploit my talent now, but I wanted him to move ahead,' she says, explaining why she repeatedly urged him to change his way of life in music.

As Annapurna Devi's student.

A young Hariprasad with Annapurna Devi; Baba Allauddin Khan in the background.

Hariprasad with a friend.

Son Rajeev and daughter-in-law Pushpanjali with Hariprasad and Anuradha.

With twin granddaughters Renee and Raaina.

Ustad Amir Khan greets Hariprasad on stage as Begum Akhtar looks on.

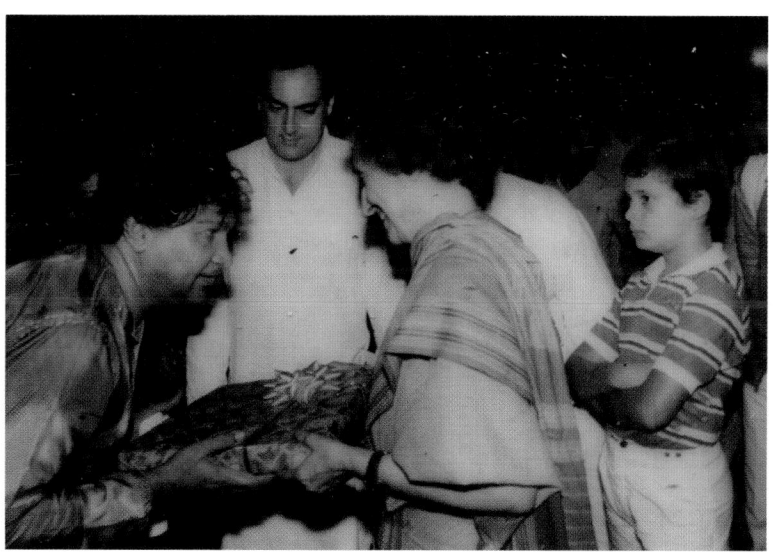

With then PM Indira Gandhi. Rajeev Gandhi looks on.

At Rotterdam. With Queen Maxima of the Netherlands.

One for the album: A signed photo from George Harrison to Hariprasad and Shiv Kumar Sharma.

The geniuses behind the still popular *Call of the Valley*—Hariprasad,
Shiv Kumar Sharma and Brijbhushan Kabra.

Cover of the LP record of *Shankar Family and Friends*.

During his film-music-recording days with singer Manna De, flautist and saxophone player Manohari-da and sitarist Acharya.

A light moment with music director C. Ramchandra.

Lost in music.

The Chaurasias: When the world was young . . .

Music without barriers: with South Korean musician Jang-Hyun Won.

Hariprasad with James Galway of the Golden Flutes.

The timelessness of music: with Ustad Zakir Hussain (above) and
Ustad Alla Rakha (below).

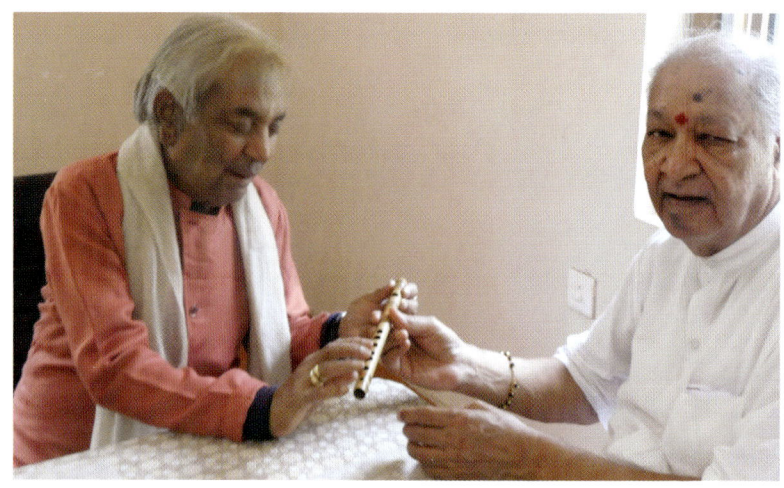

A friendship spanning decades: with Kathak maestro Birju Maharaj.

Dropping in to visit Pt Jasraj in New Jersey from New York.

With fellow flautist and saxophone player Santosh Yadav at the studio. Hariprasad often came in after artistes had rehearsed and added his melody to the composition.

At Bhubaneswar Gurukul with student Digvijay Chauhan.
The peacock is a constant presence.

With singer Suman Kalyanpur. The Chaurasias would occupy a flat in the same building in Bombay as the singer, many years later.

Accompanying the Nightingale at the Tirupati temple recitals.

With Lata Mangeshkar at the Tirupati temple, where the Lord blessed his flute.

Conducting his composition at AIR Cuttack.

Hariprasad Chaurasia with P.V. Krishnamurthy,
the AIR station director who gave him wings to compose music.

Amitabh Bachchan listens as Hariprasad explains.
Shiv Kumar Sharma and Yash Chopra look on.

Hariprasad receiving an honour from
beloved ex-president Dr Kalam, who
was a great admirer and patron of
Indian classical music.

With Ratan Tata, who made his 'dream
of having a Gurukul come true'.

The US tour group: Ravi Shankar, George Harrison, Shiv Kumar Sharma and Hariprasad
in the front row along with other musicians. Lakshmi Shankar stands behind.

Class in progress in Boxwood, Canada.

Father Pehelwan (wrestler)
Chedilal Chaurasia.

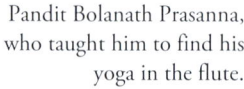

Pandit Bolanath Prasanna,
who taught him to find his
yoga in the flute.

'When my voice thickened, I decided not to perform in public any more. In Orissa, people would say, "Begum Akhtar sings with a heavy voice, Reshma has a heavy voice, why don't you sing too?" But I was not able to come to terms with the changes in my voice and control.'

Anuradha also found herself comparing her changed voice with that of her new neighbour, at Anand building on Kalakar Dhurandhar Marg in Khar, Bombay, where they moved after a few years of living in Shiv Darshan. 'I would hear Suman Kalyanpur singing, and her voice was a deterrent to my singing,' she says.

The Chaurasias moved out from Anand building after four years there, to a roomier space in Costa Belle, where they would come across an earlier neighbour from their Hotel Evergreen days— Anand Bakshi, the lyricist. But though there was no deterrent voice to compare to her own, Anuradha found she was singing only for herself. Instead, she concentrated on her husband's playing, setting herself up as commentator and critic.

Anuradha admits, 'I would often criticize him, his work. I am his sternest, severest critic. Others would scold me, but it changed nothing. I would attend all his programmes in town at least, and listen and give him feedback. I would sit while he played ragas, watch, listen, comment.'

The combined result of all the prodding from different sources leads Hariprasad to seriously consider finding a guru and immersing himself in classical music again. Recollecting the advice given to him by Baba Allauddin Khan in his childhood, he decides to seek out his daughter, Annapurna Devi. 'I learnt she lived in Pavlova, near the Hanging Gardens in south Bombay, so I took myself there to meet her,' he recalls. The year was 1966.

He stands at the door of the flat. Hesitantly, he knocks. Softly at first. Then, receiving no response, a bit louder. The door opens. He asks to meet Annapurna Devi. But when he does see her, he finds himself at a loss for words.

'Why have you come?' she asks.

'For a darshan,' he replies.

She responds with, 'Why me? Go and have a darshan of Ravi Shankar.'

He tells her about the meeting with her father, Baba Allauddin Khan, and the advice the musician had given him to learn from her. She listens to him, then is silent. He can sense she is angry. She says nothing for a long while.

'I play the surbahar, not the bansuri,' she tells him. And nothing else. He senses her rejection. And paying his respects, gets up and leaves.

As he puts it, Hariprasad would keep 'visiting her for three years and repeating my request, but she kept turning me away'. He would also notice signs of the diverse paths between Annapurna Devi and her celebrated husband. 'He would dress very differently by then, his clothes were very modern. It was obvious he was in a different world.'

The three years would see Annapurna Devi's marriage coming to an end. In 1968, along with her twenty-five-year-old son, Shubhendra, she would shift out of Pavlova and move to a small flat in Akash Ganga on Peddar Road.

'Now she would say she was busy in chores around the house, and had no time to teach me,' Hariprasad says of his visits to Annapurna Devi at Akash Ganga, 'but I persisted and kept going back.'

Much has been written about the extent of Annapurna Devi's reclusiveness in the years after 1968. Bandyopadhyay writes in his book of what he saw as he stepped out of the lift on the sixth floor of Akash Ganga Apartments: 'I saw the plastic notice board bearing her instructions about ringing the bell: how many times and on which days.'

In fact, the black plastic board read very clearly in all capital letters: PLEASE RING THE BELL ONLY THREE TIMES. IF NOBODY ANSWERS, PLEASE LEAVE YOUR CARD. THANK YOU FOR BEING CONSIDERATE. Under the instructions was the sign-off. It read: Acharya Allauddin Music Circle, 8-A Akashganga, Mumbai 400020.

He also describes his first visit to the house. Of the room he enters, he says: 'Was an ordinary room with a plain couch and a centre table. A reddish carpet was spread on the floor.'

Bandyopadhyay also cites his first impressions of his future guru, whom he notices sitting on a low stool near the entrance:

She wore a white cotton saree with a touch of mauve on the pleat and a plain white blouse. All very ordinary. She had a plastic bangle and an iron bangle wrapped in gold, one generally worn by married Bengali women on the right hand. A thick layer of vermillion shone prominently in the parting of her hair. It seemed the eyebrows were touched up with a black pencil and were thick and elongated. A small knot of hair was drawn straight backwards. The hair was moist, as if she had just taken a bath.

Hariprasad, however, a simple man himself, only sees her in the avatar of a guru.

Anuradha recalls the years Hariprasad spent persuading Annapurna Devi to be his guru. 'For three years, he would visit her two or three times a month. She would ask him questions like an inquisitor, and send him away. She was adamant but he was just as stubborn. She told him, "You already have money, and are a flautist; I play the surbahar. How can I teach you?" He told her, "I want gyan, teach me what you know in surbahar, music is music. I have come to you to learn music." When she finally started teaching, she would teach him by singing, alaap, jod, jhala, which is more vocal than instrumental. It was amazing listening to her voice. I used to go along too.'

Hariprasad remembers the day Annapurna relented. 'Finally, one day, she asked me what I did for a living. "I play in films," I told her. To my surprise, she said, "I have heard that someone plays the flute very well in films . . . so it's you!" I could see her sudden interest in me. After a long moment she said, "Let's hear something."' Hariprasad says he took out his flute and played Raga Yaman, very nervously. Annapurna Devi listened intently. 'You are already an ustad. Why do you want to learn from me?' she wanted to know. When Hariprasad responded, saying he wanted to delve into the classical, learning from the very beginning, she told him, 'I will call you—the mood and time depends on me.'

Hariprasad had to be content with that. But his tapasya was finally bearing fruit.

'I kept visiting her, to keep her promise fresh in her mind with my continued visits, and one day, she nodded and bade me sit. She was teaching her son to play the sitar, and she said, "Sit with him, see how he plays." So, I would sit and listen, watch how he played, how she was teaching him, slowly but surely making him worthy of performing. I used to also practise while he was practising. She would listen. Maybe she finally felt I could do something worthwhile in music, that I was not just filmy, and I would listen to what she had to say and teach. And she agreed to start lessons in earnest. I was overjoyed, I told her I would give up films, and sit at her feet,' Hariprasad remembers, 'but she said it was wrong to turn Lakshmi away. And told me to continue playing and taking up assignments.'

To adjust to the fact that he would be busy till late in the evening, Annapurna Devi agreed to take his lessons at night, after his film shifts were over. 'I will teach you and Subho at different times,' she said. 'Do not leave your work; come to me sometime after 1 a.m.'

That simple statement would be the beginning of the rest of Hariprasad's life.

He is now tied to a timetable of his own making. Luckily, waking up early has never been a problem for him, and he continues to wake up to pursue his morning riyaz. Then he is off to the studios, and the day sees him, more often than not, shuttling between studios and recordings. Anuradha remembers that he could do this despite a rule that an accompanist could only play in one studio per day, because music directors shut their eyes to the rule in his case. Often, his shift would end too late for him to grab a meal at home, and he would hurry to Peddar Road for his lesson.

Though a strict teacher, unrelenting in her pursuit of excellence in her own music as much as in her pupil's, Annapurna Devi would also prove a caring one. 'The first thing she would ask me when I entered the house was if I had eaten. Often she would cook for me, or make sure there was enough food for me to eat. In later years, she even made chicken curry for me, it was delicious,' says the flautist who is also known widely as a food lover. 'Sometimes there were sweets, once she learned of my weakness for sweets. She got fond of me, and never thinking about what Subho or Ravi might think of it, would sit through the night with me.'

His guru is an exacting teacher indeed. Hariprasad understands soon enough that he needs to unlearn everything he has learnt over all these years, and start afresh. For one, the flute must change. He puts away the smaller, handier bamboo flutes he has been playing, and takes up a three-foot-long instrument. 'Longer than what even Pannalal Ghosh uses,' according to Anuradha. He does admit it was a wise decision. 'The bigger flute has a low sound. The smaller flutes are higher pitched, even shrill at times. Listening to that for an hour will drive people mad,' he laughs.

The change in instrument implies relearning to play the flute. The fingering changes due to the change in distance. Though he has spoken about it in other interviews, for the book, Hariprasad is silent about whether he chose to play left-handed to prove to his guruma that he was starting his music from the beginning, or whether it was demanded of him. 'It was a new flute, so I decided to change the hand too,' is all he will say.

His new instrument was perfect for his guruma's style of teaching. She began with Yaman, which, along with Bhoop, is the starting raga for many basic students. She would demonstrate by singing. Her voice, more flexible than any instrument, would rise and fall and glide easily between notes. '"Tune yourself, blow into your flute like I am singing," she said,' Hariprasad revealed in an interview on *Art Talk* for News X.

He remembers her dismay at his first sessions. He was impatient with the alaap, and true to his years of playing for and listening to film music, would jump into the rhythm segment in a few minutes after he had begun his piece. 'She asked him, "Why do you jump like a monkey, from here to there? Take long alaaps,"' Anuradha recollects.

In *Woodwinds of Change*, Singh, who persuaded Annapurna Devi to give him a written interview, quotes her views of her gharana, which in turn influenced her own teaching style.

'Our gharana's contribution to instrumental Indian classical music is its own unique system of unfolding a raga. In the Senia–Maihar gharana, the usual style of presentation is the dhrupad. The alaaps are systematic, slow, dignified, serene, without the khataas and the murkis; the jod anga has intricate laykari, rhythmic patterns, and the alaap and jhala offer a plethora of variations. Throughout the presentation, the purity of the raga is maintained. The gats (compositions) of the Maihar gharana are not confined only to teen taal (sixteen-beat rhythmic cycle).'

Following the dhrupad style characteristic of the Maihar gharana, her alaap would be long, slow and meditative. The same style of slow exposition of the alaap that Ravi Shankar has rejected in his more recent playing as not suitable for contemporary audiences. In *Romancing the Bansuri*, a film by Rajeev Chaurasia, Hariprasad does explain the travails of following a teacher of Annapurna Devi's stature.

'The slow movement helped me, it was very difficult to adopt the style, but I got the power. Guruma's singing was very fast, and difficult to copy that speed. I also copied the surbahar.'

He had no option but to learn to do so. In fact, though he does not know it then, by following both voice and instrument, he is equipping himself with enough knowledge and technique to evolve his own path-breaking style of presenting classical music on the flute.

The lessons stretch for two, sometimes three hours, till 4 a.m. But progress is painstakingly slow. In the nature of all purist teachers of classical music, Hariprasad learns soon, his teacher too will not progress to the next step until he has perfected what she has just taught him. He patiently lets the lesson take its course. Often, he finds himself challenged, as he holds the flute away, while finding his breath. He, who prides himself on his ability to hold a note longer than most others! It makes him humble, though in his heart he knows he has no ego left; the realization that he has a sea of knowledge to cross in music has made his ego slink quietly away.

For the first time, he understands that each note has an emotion it can touch in the human mind. The same note in different ragas evokes different moods. His teacher explains it all, by example, and by making him practise. 'I would listen, learn, practise and present the music to her,' Hariprasad says, adding that his dedication must have impressed his guru, because, 'she got fond of me.'

Slowly, but surely, the lessons progress. Unstinting of her knowledge which runs deep, Annapurna imparts it to him. Patiently, and with dedication, Hariprasad learns something that Raja Ram had asked him to do, many years earlier—to use his breath to sing. 'I learnt to use the flute and my breath to express notes and taans, like in vocal music,' he says simply, underplaying the supreme effort needed to do what he has achieved.

Explaining the difficulties peculiar to flute playing, Digvijay Chauhan, one of Hariprasad's disciples at the Vrindaban Gurukul in Bhubaneswar, Orissa, says, 'Unlike other instruments, where we need to change strings to change the scale, in the flute, only breath makes the change possible. From sa to saa and to the pa in the higher octave, it is in the same scale. But it needs a lot of knowledge and technical skill to be able to go above pa in the third octave.' Skills that Hariprasad learnt as lessons picked up and his understanding of classical music deepened.

Yet, lessons were not always smooth flowing. 'Guruma was like a coconut,' Hariprasad says, 'very irritable. One could not ask her questions or interrupt her. She would get angry, as her thought would get disrupted.'

Right in the beginning of their sittings, Annapurna Devi has warned her student of the danger of asking questions. 'You will not interrupt me or ask why, but follow me unquestioningly,' she has decreed. Hariprasad has obviously forgotten, and is carried away by the fact that she has become so much more approachable with passing months.

He recounts an incident. 'Guruma was saying that music could not be like running, there was no need for speed. It had to be like prayer, *prarthana*. I interrupted her, saying, "But people like speed . . ." and there was a loud bang. "Are you learning for others or learning music?" she said and broke the tanpura on my head!'

What happened next reveals Hariprasad's nature without any need for words.

'I picked up the pieces, wrapped them carefully in cloth, and placed them at her feet,' he says, a smile lighting the memory. 'Guruma started laughing. "What madness is this?" she asked. It was obvious that she had inherited her father's mercurial temper, which would flash without warning,' he adds. 'Baba was said to have thrown a hammer at a radio artiste. He was explaining a taan, and was asked by the artiste to repeat. He threw the hammer hurting the man's head, and said, "What were you doing, sleeping? Here it is."'

Unfazed by his teacher's show of anger, knowing it was momentary, Hariprasad took the pieces of the broken instrument to Bhargava Music, who 'repaired it well, making it as good as new. They put the pieces together like a jigsaw puzzle, added polish, and you could never make out it was broken. The sound was back.'

There were other times Guruma showed her temper. He remembers, 'Like when I took homeopathic medicine for her because she had been coughing badly while teaching the previous night. She went to the window and threw the bottle out, then turned to me and asked, "Are you my doctor? You have come to learn, do that."'

Memories of his time as a student with Annapurna Devi include teaching her to drive. 'It happened quite strangely. The car was there, an Ambassador. She had got it for Subho, who was not around then. Something had needed repair and the mechanic brought the car back after the job was done and asked for his money. "Come and check," the mechanic said. "Who will drive the car to test it?" she asked him. "I can't drive." I told her then, "You must learn to start the car, and to drive. You might need to go to buy medicine."' With some persuasion, Hariprasad gets his teacher to learn to drive. And, Anuradha adds, 'He got her a licence too, without her having to give the driving test.'

Hariprasad also remembers approaching Ravi Shankar when he came to know that the sitar maestro was planning to leave his flat to Kamala, his lady love. It was soon after Annapurna Devi had moved to Akash Ganga. 'She was very disturbed, both by his leaving and by the news. I approached Ravi-ji and said, "You cannot do that!" Ravi-ji replied, "But who are you?" I told him, "I am her student, and I also respect you a lot, but I cannot see her suffer. I won't let her suffer." Ravi-ji immediately agreed to change his decision. But,' he remembers, 'when, later, Ravi-ji wanted to come back and take up the marriage threads again, she refused him.'

Hariprasad spent many years learning from Annapurna Devi. She taught him Abhogi, Jhinjhoti, Yaman, besides others. But her teaching went beyond ragas, giving him a depth of knowledge that he could use to create his own style and musical vocabulary. He learnt to speak with the flute, and reach out through his playing to touch the hearts of his audience. She also initiated him into all the lighter forms of classical music which he added to his own knowledge of folk tunes and pastoral ditties.

'She taught me every form of music—dhrupad, dhamar, tappa, thumri, kajri. I've never seen the kind of variety in any other gharana as my Guruma's Maihar gharana has,' he said in an interview to Meenakshi Sinha for the *Times of India*.

A short documentary film made for the AIR films division, titled *Hariprasad Chaurasia Demonstration and Performance*, has the flautist playing Desh against visuals of temple sculptures and miniature paintings of Radha and Krishna. The commentary describes him as 'one of our most gifted young flautists . . . whose musical thinking and style have been greatly influenced by Annapurna Ravi Shankar, wife of the great sitar player under whom Chaurasia has been training.'

It is the visual of Hariprasad that is of interest. He plays with ease, demonstrating gamak, meend and murki with no effort, not a frown disturbing his brow nor a furrow running across his forehead as his fingers create the notes and his breath, the music. Already, the teacher has begun moulding her pupil in letting the bansuri sing, expressing as much as the human voice can in words.

Ustad Zakir Hussain comments on Hariprasad's momentous achievement in the Film Division documentary, *Bansuri Guru*, made by Hariprasad's son, Rajeev Chaurasia. Zakir says that while it took the work of generations of players to achieve acceptance for newer instruments like the sarod and the sitar as classical instruments on par with the been and the veena, and even longer for the elevation of the rudraveena and the sarangi, Hariprasad has in a single lifetime lifted a folk instrument to the status of a premier classical instrument worthy and capable of performing solo concerts in classical music. He has taught the flute to play jhalas, jods, chattans, chands, tihais, all elements of Indian music, something that has never been done before.

In *An Unheard Melody*, Bandyopadhyay reports in an interview with his subject that in response to his question, 'What is so special in your teaching?' she told him, 'I do not know. I teach in such a way that men get some joy and peace of mind. I taught Hariprasad in such a way. I taught him things the flute was not fit to play. He said, "*Maa-ji, bansuri mein aisa nahin ho sakta* . . . all these things are not possible on the flute." I said, "*Jaroor hoga*, you can do it." And he was able to play all the angs played by other instruments. He has earned a name.'

Digvijay Chauhan adds that his guru's introduction of 'tonguing', a technique he teaches his students too, makes the playing unique and adds clarity, akin to a vocalist mouthing the lyrics. And Anuradha takes credit for the fact that her husband abandoned the F scale flute in favour of the E scale instrument. 'The higher pitch gave classical music a lighter feel; I recommended he play on a lower note, and that has made all the difference.'

Annapurna Devi's main contribution to every one of the musicians who sat at her feet to imbibe from her fount of knowledge lay in the fact that she instinctively knew each one's capabilities and developed their strengths and styles in a manner unique to them. 'Guruma helped me develop my style,' Hariprasad puts it simply.

'I could have learnt so much more,' he says, of his brief stint with his guru. 'Even when she was too sick to teach, I would go over and practise in front of her. If she touched my hand, it was teaching for me.'

Playing across Continents

Though the Beatles had shaken off the influence of Maharishi Mahesh Yogi, the fascination George Harrison had for Indian music, and in particular, the sitar, endured. It was well known that he considered Ravi Shankar his guru. The sitarist, in turn, keen to take his music to the West, was ready for collaborations that would take his music to an ever-widening circle of international audiences. In *Poignant Song: The Life and Music of Lakshmi Shankar*, her biographer Kavita Das writes, 'For his part Ravi was more interested in bringing Indian music together with Western traditions holistically rather than pulling out exotic motifs.'

The text goes on to say, 'Although Ravi had collaborated with large ensembles of musicians in India, he had yet to do so in the West, where he was more known as a solo musician.' He decided to bring together a group comprising the best-known names in Carnatic and Hindustani music, and with that aim in mind, he set out on a coast-to-coast tour. He also meant to record the music for commercial sales. Surprisingly, while the group included Alla Rakha on the tabla and Shivkumar Sharma on the santoor, it was Sharad Kumar who was to play the flute as well as the shehnai. Whether it was because Hariprasad was learning from Annapurna Devi, or because Ravi Shankar considered him a light music player best suited for films, the reason remains unknown.

Come 1973, the perception has changed. When Harrison, now performing as a solo entity, after the much publicized break-up of the Beatles, decides to produce and release a full studio album under his own label, Dark Horse Records, in collaboration with Ravi Shankar, the sitarist again handpicks the members of his ensemble. Singer and sister-in-law Lakshmi Shankar, tabla maestro Alla Rakha, violinist L. Subramaniam, sarangi maestro Sultan Khan, and santoor wizard Shivkumar Sharma are on board along with a plethora of other well-known artistes from both genres of music. Much-loved flautist Hariprasad Chaurasia is also a part of the troupe. As is Shankar's son, Subho. The Western team includes George Harrison as vocalist, guitarist and autoharp, keyboardist and vocalist Billy Preston, bass guitarist Klaus Voorman, drummers Jim Keltner and Ringo Starr, saxophonist Tom Scott and percussionist Emil Richards. Das writes in *Poignant Song* about the album, aptly titled *Shankar Family and Friends*, and recorded at A&M Studios in Los Angeles.

Take a look at the album cover in the archives, and the camaraderie and sense of excitement is almost palpable in the photograph. Shot formally at A&M Studios, the cover with tongue-in-cheek has all the instrumentalists playing, not their own, but instruments from the 'opposite culture'. Thus, Ravi Shankar sports a baritone saxophone, George Harrison sits behind a small drum, Keltner plays another hand drum whereas Rakha holds a pair of drumsticks, bass player Voormann has a tambura, Sharma a Western-style violin, and Chaurasia a bass flute.

Shankar Family and Friends would feature among its series of promo records the hit single '*I Am Missing You*' sung in two styles by Lakshmi Shankar—Krishna bhajans written and composed by Ravi Shankar plus the aarti bhajan '*Om Jagdish Hare*'—and carry the Dark Horse Records emblem of the Indian mythological Uchchaisravas, a galloping seven-headed stallion.

Hariprasad does not usually dwell on *Shankar Family and Friends* in his interviews. The recording that remains at the top of his list of memorable collaborations is Music Festival from India, a year later, in 1974. Once again, Ravi Shankar orchestrates the coming together of the ensemble group of artistes. Once again, Hariprasad and his flute are to play in the new project. And this time, the group would embark on a tour.

'The recording was at Harrison's home; it was a castle,' Hariprasad says, laughing at the memory. 'We stayed in a hotel opposite, and rehearsed and recorded in the castle, Fraire Park, located in Henley upon Thames, where a room had been set up as a recording studio.'

The instinctive virtuosity of Indian musicians who could collaborate harmoniously without prior preparation or rehearsal impresses the Westerners.

In *Poignant Song*, Das quotes from *Raga Mala: The Autobiography of Ravi Shankar*, where Harrison says:

> Most of the music for the album was played live in the drawing room of my house—we had mics (sic) up to the studio. Ravi would tell everybody what their part was, and Indian musicians are very good at memorizing what they have to do . . . he would go to count them in, and I thought, this is going to be chaos. But they'd start playing and it would be like magic.

The mood of the compositions was more classical, and in keeping with this, the cover of the LP record had the artistes, many in Indian clothes, sedately posing for a group photo, under the spreading branches of a tree.

The recording was a lark, Hariprasad remembers, but it is the tour that followed, usually referred to as the Dark Horse Tour, that he waxes eloquent about. 'We travelled in our own plane with an OM symbol painted on it, had cooks and istriwallas to iron our clothes, and we set off on a forty-five-city tour of Canada and America that started in Vancouver and, after travelling all over, ended in New York City.'

The musicians started by performing in Munich, Stockholm and Copenhagen as well as at the Royal Albert Hall. The London performance was a very different experience for Hariprasad from his first recital there. But it was America that Ravi Shankar and his Beatles collaborator were out to conquer. Stadiums and open-air garden venues were booked for the shows to accommodate the anticipated crowds. Hariprasad remembers with an appreciation that still colours his voice as he talks about the tour, 'We toured forty-five cities in forty-eight days. We would perform, fly, go to the hotel, rest. Then go to the stage and perform. It was like clockwork. Everything was perfectly organized. We would be given our hotel room keys on landing, our clothes would have been pressed and be hanging in the cupboard, hot food would be served to suit our tastes . . . we got Indian food everywhere. There were two trucks that were used to transport the cooks, clothes and instruments. They even tuned the instruments before every show and kept them ready so the player could begin without delay. Mine never needed tuning,' he adds mischievously.

The simple flute that does not need tuning proves capable of capturing many hearts. Hariprasad is also invited to record a solo at the same time.

The group stayed at Los Angeles after the tour, to finish Harrison's Dark Horse album. 'We stayed at Sunset Boulevard for fifteen days. Peter Sellers was there too. He would join the group on our tour whenever he was free, his girlfriend too would come along. It was fun when he was around, he knew some Indian words and would make us laugh.'

The Dark Horse Tour of the US would literally open the gates for Hariprasad. In fact, careful observers will learn that his shows overseas probably match the number of shows in India.

To date he has performed with jazz and classical artistes of the West, even teamed up to play along with the Gregorian chant. 'It has been my good fortune to have been able to associate with so many great musicians. They seemed to enjoy my music and were gracious to ask me to join them. I have never felt uncomfortable with any genre,' Hariprasad said in an interview to K. Pradeep for the *Hindu*.

He is among the first Indian soloists to perform at the Bolshoi Theatre in Moscow, as part of Days of India, a nine-day festival, organized by the Indian government in 2005. Pt Shivkumar Sharma and Dr L. Subramaniam were also part of the delegation that included folk and classical artistes.

As Surjit Singh notes in his book, 'His playing caused "appreciative riots" in the Theatre Odeon in Paris.'

From an interview by Darya Tcherkassova, press office of the Diaghilev Festival, May 2017

'This is my first visit to Perm. I have performed in Moscow and other Russian cities before. I was the first Indian musician that played in the Bolshoi Theatre. It was the year of the thirtieth anniversary of India's independence—1977. We were living in the hotel Moskva and so many people were willing to see us. Young girls and children were welcoming us with songs of Raj Kapoor. (Mr Chaurasia hummed the song 'Awaara hoon' from the famous 1951 movie *Awaara*, meaning vagabond.) That was a beautiful time that I enjoyed really. I used to love listening to Russian folk music. I even took recordings of local musicians. Their singing was astonishing—no instruments, just the voice. There is soul in that. That is the real music. Russia was real, without American influence. Now people have changed a little bit. But their interest in Indian culture is growing. I have students from Russia. They are very, very good and pick up so well. They love the Indian language, music and food. Indian cuisine is becoming popular in Russia. Even here in Perm, my group enjoyed a meal yesterday at an Indian restaurant not far from our hotel Ural. Russians love India. And in India, we love Russia.'

An Interlude

Hariprasad shares a special memory.

'I think it was in 1996. I was performing in Paris. After the show, I was approached by some local musicians who wanted to understand more about sur. I played a bit with them, it was interesting. Then added pakhavaj to the flute, and cello and violin, and gave them the notation of a composition of mine. I had composed it while [being] stuck doing nothing during the Easter break at Rotterdam, and Henri Tournier, my student from France, had got some classical musicians to add to it. I gave them the notation and they were very happy.'

The 'local musicians' would combine with Tournier, who was also assisting Hariprasad at Rotterdam, and work on the composition for two years. In 1999, during his visit to Germany, they would finally showcase the results of their work.

'We used a room behind the theatre to practise and for rehearsals. There was a lot of energy, and enthusiasm. The theatre owner was a friend, so I told him, let's do a show, I want to do this. He agreed, and said go ahead. We had two performances of *Adi Anant*, and both were houseful shows.'

In a video clip of the performance organized by the Navras Records at the Royal Festival Hall, London, the ensemble presents a colourful picture. Hariprasad and the Western flautist, along with the tabla player, are sitting cross-legged on the floor. The string instrument players, including the harpist and the horn players, occupy leather-upholstered seats or chairs as required, while the drums are on the highest tier. The piano stands facing the group on one side. The group performed Sandhya Shree, as an example of crossover music.

The *Adi Anant* compositions include six songs: two in Raga Kalyan, followed by Sandhya Shree, Kalaranjani, Bhimpalasi and Bhairavi. Kalaranjani was a raga created by Hariprasad, in which he blended Kalavati and Shivaranjani, and added both versions of ga, the flat from Shivaranjani and the regular ga from Kalavati in the avaroha, mixing the ragas to create a new, modern twist.

Later, the live music recording was released as an LP under the same name. The performers were listed as Hariprasad Chaurasia and L'Orchestre Transes Europeennes.

The Shiv–Hari Magic

By 1980, when Yash Chopra launches *Silsila*, his composers have established themselves worldwide as classical musicians who are masters of their instruments.

Considered a casting coup at the time, the film with Amitabh Bachchan, Jaya Bachchan and Rekha in the leading roles was a love story of star-crossed lovers. Shashi Kapoor and Sanjeev Kumar had roles too—one as Jaya's screen lover who dies, leaving her unmarried and pregnant, when the plane he pilots crashes just before their wedding, and the other as Rekha's husband who watches helplessly as his wife romances her former flame.

As the story goes, Amitabh marries Jaya to save her honour and his brother's name, and jilts Rekha who goes into a huff and marries Sanjeev Kumar. Not unexpectedly, the lovers are heartbroken at the turn of events. When chance brings them together again, the spark reignites, and their love story picks up once more. This in turn breaks their respective spouses' hearts, but neither seems able to do anything about it.

Things come to a head when the lovers decide to elope. But destiny intervenes when Sanjeev is involved in a plane crash, and his wife and her lover are able to witness the carnage from a helicopter in which they are flying away into their happily-ever-after. Decency and moral rectitude win over love, and the distraught Rekha reunites with her husband, and Jaya gets her man back.

Given the twists and turns in the story, and Yash Chopra's capacity for creating visual poetry, the film presented enough scope for songs.

Shivkumar Sharma goes back to the time when *Silsila* was being announced, and they had just been signed on as music directors for the film. 'There was a lot of criticism at the time, with people asking why classical musicians were being asked to score music; were we diluting our art for commercial reasons? We realized we had to rise to the occasion. We spent many sessions with Yash-ji, discussing situations, locations, story. He gave us the screenplay which we read carefully. We asked for two weeks, and sat together at home and composed the songs. Sahir was contacted to write the songs, but he was not able to fit himself into the schedule. So, after a lot of consideration, Javed Akhtar was taken on. It was his first assignment as a film writer.'

Most directors may have hesitated before or worried after signing three new talents to work on the music, but Yash Chopra has decided to take the gamble. He agrees to the large assortment of instruments that the music directors want. While the flute and the santoor have their pride of place in the compositions, the role of other instruments in creating the mood and melody is not ignored either.

Shiv–Hari now bring in their own innovations. Hariprasad suggests Amitabh should sing. '*Allahabad ka hai, use gava diya, jaise gale me haat dal ke,*' he recollects. The song they wanted him to sing was a Hori. 'Then Yash-ji suggested, "Ask his father to write the song, a UP-style Hori." We asked Amitabh, he was happy. Harivanshrai-ji was in Bombay at that time, so he was requested. Within an hour, the song was written, adapted from a song sung in rural UP. He wasted no time at all, especially since his son was to sing it,' Hariprasad says, laughing.

He remembers the hard work that Amitabh put in before the recording. 'He practised it well; the singing, movements, everything.

And he got the inflections perfectly.' '*Rang barse*', which is heard on every loudspeaker across India on Holi, has long outlived the film. It is a dramatic moment in the film, where a slightly tipsy-with-bhang Amitabh throws caution to the winds and lets everyone within earshot know that he and Rekha are lovers. The dramatic twist comes from the fact that both Jaya and Sanjeev are also listening to the Hori-ditty-turned-confession, and squirming with embarrassment.

'Whether it is an ad film of thirty seconds or a full-fledged song number, he would work hard on all of it,' Hariprasad says of Amitabh Bachchan. 'He has earned his status because of this combination of talent and hard work.' Coming from a man who spent nights learning music after a full day's work, and who practises on his flute for hours on end, this is praise indeed.

The other Amitabh song, '*Neela aasman so gaya*', is tougher. 'We had planned two versions, one by Lata, the other by Amitabh. We gave him a low base so it would be easier, and would also bring out the pathos in his voice. It worked.' Incidentally, the song developed from a tune Amitabh was humming. Snatches from a song reportedly shared by Shammi Kapoor. In the master flautist's words, 'I liked the sound of the tune, told him to sing it to us, and developed it into a full-fledged song.'

Shivkumar Sharma has a story to tell on the duet, '*Yeh kahan aa gaye hum*'. 'It was not a song situation at all; Yash-ji wanted words, poetry, set to music. We suggested a song, and that poetic verses come in between the song, instead of interlude music. First the *sthayi*, then the recitation, then the *antara*, then words again.'

The suggestion worked. Yash Chopra shot a hauntingly beautiful sequence with the santoor throbbing in the background before the other instruments join in; the music and lyrics adding layers of emotion as the poetic words speak of the hero's sense of hopelessness and despairing love. The words, spoken by Amitabh in his deep baritone drenched with emotion, made theatregoers wonder if he was speaking of his own life. The verses he was reciting of course were also by Javed Akhtar, excerpted from *Banjara*, his collection of poems.

When the director needed to give Jaya a song, he decided on a Meera bhajan, '*Jo tum todo piya*'.

'He wanted Lata-ji to sing it of course; she sang in all his films. I told Yash-ji, "Lata may not sing this song, she has decided not to sing Meera bhajans except for her brother Hridaynath's compositions."' Yash-ji said, "Let's see." So we went ahead and composed the tune. We kept it classical, in Bhairavi.'

An Interlude

Shiv–Hari are recording 'Dekha ek khwab' for Silsila. They are aware that the song is picturized on Amitabh and Rekha, who are cavorting among the breathtaking tulip gardens of Keukenhof in the Netherlands, alternating with the misty landscape of Pahalgam, Kashmir. The tune is light, romantic, the seventy-piece orchestra is in perfect sync, and Kishore Kumar and Lata Mangeshkar are giving it just the right lift with their voices.

Song over, the directors sit back to listen, to see if everything sounds the way they want it to. They know it will, but as first-time music directors and for a big banner at that, there is no harm of course in being doubly sure.

It is Lata's habit to leave immediately after her recording. Her days are so busy, she cannot but do so. And anyway, over the years, she has sung and recorded enough songs to know that it has gone just right.

But today, she is still in the studio. She seems relaxed as she listens to the playback. All through. If Hariprasad or Shivkumar are surprised, they do not show it. Instead, they realize they have been presented with an opportunity.

'Was it good?' they ask Lata, though they are sure of her response. The singer says she likes the song. That is when Shivkumar takes his chance. 'There is another song we would like you to sing. It is filmed on Jaya-ji, and is a dramatic moment in the film. But,' he adds, 'it is a Meera bhajan. We have composed the tune in Bhairavi.'

To their surprise and delight, Lata agrees to sing it. It is perhaps the only time she made a concession and broke her self-imposed diktat about Meera bhajans.

Just for the record, the Meera bhajan, *'Jo tum todo piya'*, was being used for the third time in Hindi films. Vasant Desai had created the first song on Meerabai's lyrics, in Bhairavi, for V. Shantaram's dance-based *Jhanak Jhanak Payal Baaje*. The song had been sung by Lata when the heroine is thrown out of her house and lives like a sanyasin in a temple hermitage. The second time, for Gulzar's *Meera*, the song was filmed on Hema Malini, and sung by Vani Jairam, as by then Lata had decided not to sing Meera bhajans for other composers. Pt Ravi Shankar had set the words to music. Also in Bhairavi, the sitar is prominent in the Meera composition. Shiv–Hari set the song in Bhairavi, and as Meera imagines that Krishna has withdrawn from her life, which is the crux of the song, the flute is absent too, and only the santoor joins the orchestra which provides a subdued backing.

The song was clipped out of the film before release, but was retained in the records.

Hariprasad adds, 'Even before *Silsila*, Yash-ji had offered us *Kala Patthar*. We turned it down. Rajesh Roshan was already working on the music; he had even composed a few songs. The film had stalled for a while and when he started on it again, Yash-ji offered it to us. But Rajesh is Roshan's son, we had played for him, and cannot snatch a film from anybody, let alone another music director's child.'

When it is released in 1981, *Silsila* ends up as one of Yash Chopra's few flops. Despite the stellar cast and the much-loved music, it does poorly at the box office. Filmgoers expecting to see an on-screen delineation of the Amitabh–Jaya–Rekha triangle that movie magazines were going on about, felt cheated by a cooked-up love story that, while entertaining, only proved that fact could be more powerful than fiction. It would take years for wiser cinema fans to see the film as a movie without drawing real-life parallels, and discover it afresh. The music, however, remained untouched by the ups and downs, and can be heard even today.

Silsila marks the beginning of a long relationship between Yash Chopra and Shiv–Hari. It also establishes the composer duo as musicians who make the classical approachable, much as Ravi Shankar, Naushad, S.D. Burman, Anil Biswas and other music directors of the 1960s had done. Their knack for creating songs derived from the folk tradition or based on classical ragas that they steeped in melody make their compositions hummable as well as memorable. *Silsila* was followed by a line of other films by Yash Chopra, all the way down to the 1990s.

Their next collaboration, *Faasle*, true to Chopra's oeuvre, was another love story. Blending two generations into a complex pattern, the story has Rekha and Sunil Dutt paired together along with two newcomers, Farah (now better known as Tabu's sister) and Rohan, singer Mahendra Kapoor's son. The director ticked all the boxes with this one. Lovely locales, star-crossed lovers, high-strung drama, and yet the movie did not get him an audience. The music by Shiv–Hari, too, was somehow not on par with the songs they had composed for *Silsila*. Neither did the littérateur poet Shaharyar's lyrics rise to the level of the ghazals and nazms he had written for *Umrao Jaan*. '*Hum chup hai ke*', in its happy and sad versions, enjoyed some favour, but neither version is heard today.

The nine songs of *Faasle* include a *bidaai* song, sung by Shobha Gurtu and Pamela Chopra. And in '*Chandni tu hai kahan*', the scene, though reminiscent of '*Neela aasman*', does not have the same impact. It is only in '*In aakhon ke zeenon se*', set on a lake in Switzerland, that the song picturization and the music seem to come together. The santoor creates the right mood, while the crossing of the two sets of lovers in their respective boats, creates a certain tension. Incidentally, *Faasle* was Chopra's first shooting experience in Switzerland. He would follow it up with so many more location shoots in that country, that the Swiss Tourism board now has a dedicated Yash Chopra tour for Indian tourists.

Even as they continue their classical pursuits, playing at programmes for Indian and international audiences, and for the radio, Shiv–Hari's links with Yash Chopra stay strong. They compose for his next film, which, sadly, does not do well either. *Vijay* sinks like a torpedoed boat despite a storyline borrowed from *Trishul*, and a star cast that includes Rishi Kapoor, Anil Kapoor, Meenakshi Seshadri, Sonam, Moushumi Chatterjee, Rajesh Khanna, Gulshan Grover, and a host of 'baddies', among others.

Two beautiful numbers survive from this celluloid debacle. '*Meri aanken hain aapki aankhen*' has a poignancy in the notes and lyrics to match, while the picturization of the double duet sung by Suresh Wadkar and Lata Mangeshkar, '*Badal pe chal ke aa*', has the Shiv–Hari stamp of melody combining with off-the-beaten-track lyrics by Nida Fazli.

Both Yash Chopra and the Shiv–Hari team would strike gold and score a surefire hit with *Chandni*.

Dismissing tried-and-tested family feuds, and multi-starrers that had refused to shine, Chopra decides on a romantic triangle. It is after all his favourite subject, and most suited to his style of filmmaking. He selects Sridevi, known for her dancing skills, whose talent he believes will do justice to the role he has eked out for her as the lead around whom the story will revolve. It is a gamble once again, because the country has been enslaved by another powerhouse of talent named Amitabh Bachchan, who, as the angry young man, has pushed romance and music right out of Hindi films.

Chopra has signed on Rishi Kapoor and Vinod Khanna as the other two vertices of the triangle, acting as foils to each other in the unfolding drama. The story ensures there is enough scope for a variety of music, from wedding numbers to love songs, happy duets to sad solos. Adding to the usual duets between lovers, he includes a song between Chandni's two suitors, where they describe their beloveds without realizing they are describing the same woman. It is not the first time the idea has been used in films. *Mere Mehboob* had

Sadhana and Ameeta singing praises of their respective heart-throbs, who happened to be one and the same—Rajendra Kumar.

After a tumultuous, whirlwind romance that leads to an engagement and general joy on all sides, tragedy strikes when Rishi Kapoor is crippled in an accident. Despite Sridevi's beautiful song offering to share his pain, the hero plays gallant and refuses to let her ruin her life by marrying a cripple. Heartbroken, Sridevi snuffs out her exuberance and takes up a job. But her sedate beauty is a magnet for her boss, who woos her and takes her home to his mother, and convinces Sridevi to be his bride.

In true Yash Chopra fashion, coincidences abound in *Chandni* too. The two men meet, become friends, even sing a song as they trade confidences and extol the virtues of their beloved. One coincidence leads to another, and Rishi Kapoor lands at Chandni's place. Another round of broken hearts, songs, and finally, a happy ending for the hero and heroine, while the third man suffers in silence, with even the audience forgetting about him.

Discovering that the twists and turns allowed enough scope, Shiv–Hari mined their talents and created nine songs. Anand Bakshi, who was writing the lyrics, rose magnificently to the occasion.

The film created a stir even before it was completed. The music would create a bigger stir. Everything from Sridevi's clothes to her mannerisms were adopted by her fans. Yash Chopra had created a superstar with *Chandni*.

Knowing he had a winner in Shiv–Hari's music compositions, the director released the soundtrack in advance. According to Yash Raj Films, 'the soundtrack went four times Platinum by the day of the premiere. By the twenty-fifth week, it went twenty-five times Platinum, a new standard in the music industry at that time.' It reportedly holds the seventy-second place among the all-time great soundtracks of Hindi cinema.

Of the songs of *Chandni*, perhaps the ones most representative of Shiv–Hari's musical style is '*Mere haathon mein*', a sangeet occasion song that showcases Sridevi's dancing skills perfectly even as it focuses on her expressive face and large eyes. The music is true to the occasion, and uses the dholak for the rhythm with violins and other instruments creating just the right band baaja sound associated with weddings. Little wonder that the song remains a wedding favourite even today.

In '*Aa meri jaan*', a melodious blend of flute and santoor support a song created in the seductive mujra tradition, as is also evident from Sridevi's mode of dress for the scene. The filmmaker gives it a clever slant by making it an offering of love and sharing to a man dejected by his disability.

But it is in '*Mitwa*' that the film finds possibly its most successful number. The flute prelude set against the backdrop of a Swiss hamlet is pure Hariprasad, and is still popular with students of the flute as well as the piano. The Internet has many sites spelling out the *sargam* as the first step to learning to play the tune. The beat of silver anklets adds a romantic side. Again, striking out for variety within a known format, the interludes are each different from the other. The first interlude has the flute coming in, the second has the santoor, and in the third, a chorus of voices sings before the two instruments join to take the song into the next stanza.

And then there is '*Chandni*', the title song. With a story of its very own.

An Interlude

Shiv–Hari are working on the title song. And it is proving more difficult than they expected it to be. When Sridevi told them she wished to sing a song, just as Amitabh Bachchan had done in *Silsila*, the musicians were happy. Having the heroine involved in a song would mean that she got involved in the picture too. 'I have promised my father I will sing in this film,' she has told them. And they have worked to ensure she has a duet in the film.

But the recording is another story. Sridevi realizes how difficult it is to face the microphone. The singing, the coordination with Jolly Mukherjee, the male singer, everything makes her want to give up.

The director, as is his habit, is present at the time. Chopra is fully involved in all the recordings, and this one is special. Once the first rehearsal is over, there is a discussion on how the situation can be salvaged. In Hariprasad's words, 'We added words and exclamations, and it made everything easier for her.' However, the story of the recording does not end quite so simply. Sridevi listens eagerly to the final take and is unhappy with it. Chopra sanctions another recording. The entire exercise is repeated. This time the star is more comfortable with the microphone, and the recording is smoother. The song goes on to become a hit, thanks to the 'salvaging' and the excellent picturization. In fact, the *Hindustan Times* ranks it as one of the five best Yash Chopra songs. As for Sridevi, in *Chandni*, her fans cannot get enough of her, and simply overlook her somewhat shrill singing.

Chandni wins for its producer–directors the National Award for its 'clean and wholesome entertainment'. And Filmfare awards cinematographer Manmohan Singh 'the black lady' for the film's visuals. Though Shiv–Hari along with practically the entire main cast, and the producer–director too, are nominated for the Filmfare Awards, none of them win. Strange, for a film that has earned the reputation of being 'one of the most-watched films of Indian cinema'.

With *Lamhe*, Shiv–Hari hit the highest point of their stint as music directors for films. Each of the film's songs was a hit, and their range spanned the entire spectrum, from folksy numbers to romantic duets to bhajans, including a pure instrumental piece that speaks without words. Once again, Anand Bakshi wrote the lyrics for the songs.

Knowing that he had created a hit formula that could be repeated with variations to fill the box-office cash boxes, Yash Chopra incorporated many elements from *Chandni* into *Lamhe*. If *Chandni* had one wedding song and dance number, *Lamhe* had two dance numbers based on folk tunes, and set in the desert. Ila Arun's sultry voice joined Lata Mangeshkar's to good effect, and Sridevi danced with abandon to keep the viewers' eyes glued to the screen. If in '*Morni baga mein*', the audience saw Sridevi dressed in much the same manner as in '*Mere haathon mein*', with minor variations, and found her even repeating some of the actions from the earlier song, nobody minded. The music and choreography matched perfectly, and delivered the required punch.

Shiv–Hari too took a leaf out of *Chandni*, unfurling a theme tune from that film into a full-fledged duet, '*Kabhi main kahoon*', filmed on Sridevi and Anil Kapoor in *Lamhe*.

Once again, Lata was teamed to sing with a plethora of male voices. This time, Hariharan and Suresh Wadkar were signed on to sing for Anil Kapoor and Deepak Malhotra, respectively.

Yash Chopra added a parody, where a medley of songs creates a fun moment in a film that has many twists and turns bordering on high drama. While in most of the numbers, Sridevi, Anupam Kher and others dance to the music, the one remarkable segment is when Waheeda Rehman dances to '*Aaj phir jeene ki tamanna hai*', her hit song from *Guide*.

Guide would also inspire another segment of the film. When Shiv–Hari decide to create an instrumental number that would express emotions through dance, Chopra tells Sridevi to watch Waheeda in the *Guide* snake dance, to study how the senior actress expresses emotions through face and body. To her credit, choreographer Saroj Khan creates a completely modern sequence without borrowing anything from Sohanlal's creation for *Guide*, and the picturization too is uniquely *Lamhe*. Sridevi, on her part, executes the scene with gusto.

Reported to be among the '10 Best Romantic Movies of 100 years', during the Centenary Celebrations of Indian Cinema, *Lamhe* would push the boundaries, much as *Silsila* had done. But, while in *Silsila*, Chopra wound the loose ends into a safe and happy ending with the married lovers returning to their respective spouses, in *Lamhe*, Honey Irani and Dr Rahi Masoom Raza delivered a script that allowed no such neat resolution. In *Lamhe*, the happy ending, in which a much older Anil Kapoor confesses his love for his dead beloved's daughter, somehow did not go down well with the public. Perhaps, Anil Kapoor as the man who never won Sridevi but pined incessantly for her was convincing beyond his own expectation, or perhaps the audience bought too deeply into the story of unrequited love, but the fact is that they smelt incest in the love between the younger Sridevi and Anil Kapoor. Of course there was none, as the younger Sridevi was another man's daughter. But, except in a few metros and overseas, the film failed to reap the returns that *Chandni* had done.

The film, despite its mixed response, is nominated for a plethora of awards, and wins the Best Film Award for Chopra at the Filmfare Awards. It wins Sridevi a much-expected Best Actress Award, and

Anupam Kher wins the Best Supporting Actor Award. Honey Irani and Dr Rahi Masoom Raza win for story and dialogue. When the National Film Awards are announced, designer Neeta Lulla gets the National Award for Best Costume Design.

Shiv–Hari, though nominated again, do not win this time either, despite the thundering sales the music record has achieved. Not that it fazes the duo whose classical soirees keep them well and truly busy.

They continue to perform, sometimes separately, other times as a duo, across the world. And nothing speaks more eloquently of Hariprasad's love for his 'elder brother' than the fact that he spontaneously composed a raga in his honour, while touring Germany, and played it in concert as an offering to his friend in Stuttgart in the late 1980s. Called Shivanjali, the offering is implicit in the name of the raga, and is a personal acknowledgement of their friendship and collaboration as musicians.

An Interlude

It is a tense scene. Sridevi, playing Pooja the daughter, has just confessed her love for Anil Kapoor, who is still pining for his lost love, Pooja's dead mother. He goes into a rage, and hoping to bring her to her senses, slaps her. Not once. Not twice, but three times. Hard.

Chopra wants her to react to show her disappointment and anger. The options are a song, or loud music that reflects the turmoil in her heart and the clanging of mixed emotions. But Shiv–Hari want to think it through and do something different, something that will express what Chopra wants to show, yet avoid the clichés that are part of Hindi cinema vocabulary in such situations. 'We searched for an artistic way of depicting the scene,' Hariprasad recalls. 'We created a score that would let her dance Bharatanatyam in anger, and it worked.'

The '*Moments of Rage*' orchestration starts with the thudding of drums that builds up as Sridevi runs out into the open and falls to the ground on her knees. Her anguish is clear, as the mridangam beats join in, before a quick flashback to the three slaps which intercept the instruments. A heartbeat length of silence, and the scene shifts from the outdoors to a studio with Sridevi in a black skirt dress and tights. Western instruments now take up the beat in a staccato rhythm, while Sridevi dances across the screen against lighted windows. Her face and body express her mood clearly, and the music rises to be punctuated by the flashback of the three slaps, this time twice in quick succession. Wind instruments join in and take the composition to a crescendo till, exhausted, Sridevi falls to the floor. It is a masterly composition and Chopra ensures it finds its rightful place in the record and cassettes released by HMV.

Although they score three films in the years following *Chandni*, only *Darr* survives in public memory as much for its storyline and filming as for the music. The other two films, *Parampara* and *Sahibaan* have disappeared.

Darr would find Chopra carving out a thriller which would again turn the focus on an emerging superstar. Shah Rukh Khan, as the collegian who has a crush on his college mate, Juhi Chawla, and stalks her to her home, and even on her honeymoon, proved his mettle as an actor by outshining the hero, Sunny Deol. The story of *Darr*, quite linear in the unfolding, had many Yash Chopra elements, including Anupam Kher for the comic relief, Shiv–Hari for the music, Manmohan Singh handling the camera, and extensive scenes shot in Switzerland. Breaking away from the romantic theme, *Darr* would include a rather violent fight scene between hero and villain as its climax, and some scenes would have nail-biting suspense.

Without a doubt, *Darr* was a thundering hit, which was remade in Oriya and Telugu. Besides the National Film Award for Best Popular Film Providing Wholesome Entertainment, it was nominated in eight categories at the 39th Filmfare Awards, including Best Director for Chopra, Best Actress for Chawla, Best Actor for Deol, and Best

Villain for Khan, but it won two awards: Best Comedian for Kher and Best Cinematography for Manmohan Singh.

On their part, Shiv–Hari would deliver yet another winner, which would be the second bestselling soundtrack album of 1993. Estimates say that if it were valued in today's terms, the sales achieved at that time worth 10.8 crore rupees would now amount to 58 crores.

Perhaps because they are primarily instrumentalists who know their way with instruments, they compose a purely instrumental composition this time too. The scene depicts Shah Rukh Khan swinging in a hammock, alone in his living room, playing a tune on the harmonica. Innocent enough, but for the fact that there are screens surrounding him that flash larger-than-life images of Juhi Chawla. The harmonica gives way to rhythm as Juhi fills the screen, dancing to the beat. Quick changes of clothes and movements imply it is all Shah Rukh's imagination at work. The music is fast and heady, with the santoor providing one long moment of soft relief. Titled 'Obsession', the composition is completely different from the earlier instrumental pieces in Chandni and Lamhe, and perfectly suited to the scene. As Chaurasia explains, 'We listen to the situation, if possible watch the scenes, and compose accordingly. We choose the instruments to match the mood and often let silence also speak. Even silence has a role to play.' As the composition draws to an end, it blends into the villain's theme song, 'Tu hai meri Kiran'.

'Tu hai meri Kiran', the theme song of Darr, with its implied menace, goes on to become a superhit. It plays like a leitmotif through the film, much as Jackie's flute does in Hero, but here, the song grips the imagination with its unholy mix of threat with romance, as the scenes unfold. In fact, any girl who has been stalked can identify with Juhi's fear and panic on-screen, which the song evokes. The tune is racy and Udit Narayan's voice brings the right touch of longing in the antaras. The repetitive line, 'Tu hai meri Kiran' adds the hint of obsession.

In 'Ang se ang lagana', a Holi number, Shiv–Hari go rustic to create music that is both melodious and rhythmic. The scene takes the story forward, as Shah Rukh has followed Kiran to her home, and now enters the scene disguised as the drummer of a wandering band. The main tune takes a detour as he breaks into '*Rang barse*' from *Silsila*, and the chorus joins in, before going back to the original song. Using a variety of percussion instruments, including the dholak, the drum and the mridangam, the song is a foot-tapper.

The film's other hit song, where Shah Rukh imagines Juhi reciprocating his love and sings '*Tu mere samne, main tere samne*', is triggered when he hears the words being whispered to Juhi by Sunny, while they are dancing close. This song is again a fast-paced number, with a relentless rhythm that changes mood and pace suddenly when Juhi sings her responses. The quick shifts are perfectly blended, and even when, at one point, a piano is introduced, the tune holds its mood and beat. Even as Juhi changes her clothes with every few lines, with practised Miss India ease, creating picture-perfect visuals against the Swiss landscape, the underlying knowledge that this is another play-out of a stalker's obsessive dreaming as well as his possessive, sexual gestures, adds drama to the music.

Shivkumar's santoor features mainly in the love duets between Juhi and Sunny, and makes a surprise entrance in the mandatory sangeet song and dance number which has wonderfully audacious lyrics by Anand Bakshi quite in keeping with traditional Indian norms. '*Ishq ka rog bura*' is another catchy song, but one seldom heard.

In *Sahibaan*, with Madhuri Dixit, Sanjay Dutt and Rishi Kapoor in lead roles, Shiv–Hari relied on folk tunes to match the pastoral setting. The title song by Anuradha Paudwal and Jolly Mukherjee has the familiar folk lilt in it. But the classical feel of '*Prem hai deepak raga*' by Afroz Banu sets it apart. '*Bansuri yeh bansuri nahin*' by Hariharan, with lyrics after Hariprasad's own heart, recalls the magic of *Call of the Valley* as the santoor and flute play in harmony in a simple, hummable tune.

Parampara, which was released soon after *Faasle*, was directed by Yash Chopra for an outside banner. The movie, again a rehash of *Trishul*, failed miserably. Shiv–Hari did embellish it with some melodious numbers, but they went down with the film and mostly remain unheard.

An Interlude

Janmashtami, marking the birth of Krishna the flute-bearer, is approaching. Hariprasad looks at the idol of Krishna that stands in a little shrine that Anuradha has set up on the terrace of his new home, Savitri, on 19th road, Khar. The idol seems to embody the ideal he is seeking both in his life and in his music. He does not involve himself in the rituals linked to worship, but has been feeling a need for some symbolic gesture on his part to present as an offering.

I have received so much from you, Krishna, he thinks, but given back nothing . . . what can I offer you to show my gratitude . . .

The answer, when it comes, stuns him with its simplicity. He will play for the Lord, on Janmashtami, ushering in the infant Krishna from the midnight hour of his birth and celebrating his arrival through a twenty-four-hour cycle.

It is an ambitious offering, but when he embarks on it, there is a lightness in his heart, as if he is airborne.

He starts at the stroke of midnight, sitting cross-legged in front of the shrine, and as he plays, eyes closed, as if in true meditation, the hours fly past and dawn breaks. A short break to bathe and change into fresh clothes for the day, and he is back, playing. During his brief breaks, Rupak takes over, or Ramakant, whose flute, Anuradha remembers, 'was so sweet that he was Lata-ji's favourite'.

The practice continues. Over the years, as the number of his students swelled, more of them would join in, and take turns playing with him, and filling in for him, when he took his breaks. 'The celebration had taken on a larger form by the time I got married,' his daughter-in-law Pushpanjali remembers. 'The puja set-up would begin an hour or two before midnight, and many artistes, including the likes of Devaki Pandit-ji and Shekhar Sen, would come and offer bhajans. Shivkumar-ji never fails to be present. At midnight, once the aarti was over, Babuji would sit down and start playing. His students would join. And at 6 a.m., when he got up to freshen up for the day, Rupak would take over, or Rakesh . . . it was all a tacit understanding among them, but the music would never stop or flag, and the pattern still continues.'

Anuradha details how, over the years, the celebration swelled in scope, with more and more joining in. 'The door would have to be kept open, there would be people up till the steps. I would not know some of them, and think they were known to Hari-ji, only to discover later that he did not know who they were, either. But they would come, listen and leave after taking prasad. A senior pandit of the Siddhivinayak Temple in Dadar who, at the age of seventy-five, was learning to play the flute, would also come, and it was wonderful to hear the place resound with his recitation of mantras.'

Once he shifted to the Gurukul, the celebrations started being held at the large hall that houses the idols of Krishna and Radha. 'It is a huge event now, and people look forward to it, and the tradition of making an offering of the song of the flute for twenty-four hours, nonstop, continues. Today, almost sixty to seventy students join in and play,' Pushpanjali says.

An astounding fact is that despite his breathless schedule that has him jetsetting from one country to another around the year, Hariprasad ensures he is back in Bombay to play for Krishna on Janmashtami. According to Anuradha, 'There are times when I have fetched him from the airport, and he will rush to bathe and change and by midnight, take his place in front of the mandir, and start playing. Last year, I suggested we scale down the celebrations in view of his health, but he was adamant, and wants to keep everything on the same scale.'

In fact, since the Bhubaneswar gurukul was established, once the twenty-four-hour offering in Bombay is completed, Hariprasad flies to Bhubaneswar to celebrate Janmashtami with another twenty-four-hour session of flute-playing. He starts at 6 p.m. the day after he reaches, and continues till the next evening.

It comes as no surprise, then, that the flautist is a favourite with spiritual leaders, ranging from the head of the Ramkrishna Mission to Baba Ramdev, all of whom invite him to play on special occasions.

Yet Another Story

Although he has scant faith in rituals, and little time to visit temples or think of going on pilgrimages, he is winding his way up the steep hairpin-bend roads that cross seven hills to reach the richest temple in India in Tirumalai. It pleases him to note the tree-covered slopes that stretch into the distance.

He is happy Lata-ji has asked him to come along, to accompany her when she sings at the temple. Ravi Date and Mahavir, who is a music director, are also there as accompanists—Date on the tabla, Mahavir on the harmonium.

He had not expected it, but the temple town is clean, and he is impressed by the wide roads and the line-up of shops selling religious mementos. He has heard that getting a darshan of Lord Venkateshwara is never easy; the crowds of people across all ages and stations of life cause long queues that stretch for kilometres. Some wait days and sometimes return without being granted so much as a glance at the deity.

He does not have to worry. Lata-ji has been conferred with the title Asthaan Sangeet Vidhwaan Sarloo, which appoints her as the holy shrine's court musician. She has been asked to sing before the deity. In preparation, the authorities have strung up loudspeakers all over the temple township, so other pilgrims too can hear her song.

The queues have been held back, all darshan has been stopped for the occasion, to be restarted after the newly appointed shrine musician pays her respects to Lord Venkateshwara. The Lord, they are told, is waiting. They enter through the high portals of the ancient temple, the cool waters that flow along the threshold washing their feet as they step in. Through the main courtyard, into the enclosed space, and then they are in the long corridor that leads to the sanctum sanctorum.

He senses his heart hushing in awe. The idol is decorated in diamonds and flowers, the jewellery glistens in the light of the large oil lamps that shine steadily around. He realizes the four of them are alone in the presence of a God who gives a fleeting darshan to thousands of devotees every day. And yes, there are a few priests around, most probably the most senior serving at the temple.

He holds out his flute to one of them, asking for it to be placed at the feet of the Lord. *If Krishna can bless his instrument* . . . The priest shakes his head, nothing can sully the blessed feet. He asks again, and once more his request is turned down. He crosses his arms, his right hand clutching the flute still. 'If the Lord will not bless my flute, I cannot play.' It is a simple way to avoid a battle of egos, yet get the blessing he wants.

Lata and the others look nonplussed. The priests stare, disbelieving, then go into a huddle. Finally, one of them comes up, holds out his hand for the flute and walking up to the idol, places it momentarily at the golden feet. Hariprasad feels a joy he cannot describe as he holds the flute when it is handed back to him.

The Artiste as Guru

'I came into the world empty-handed, but got everything. Name, fame, money . . . I felt the need to create something that would help those who wanted to learn the flute, sincerely, to do so. I was inspired by the gurukul in Maihar that Annapurna, my guru, had. I wanted something like that.' He knew what he wanted to create. He knew it would be called 'Vrindaban', not 'Hariprasad Chaurasia', but he had no idea where the wherewithal for it would come from, or how to go about setting it up.

'For any student who is truly interested in learning or has a God-gifted talent he wants to perfect through learning, the best way is to surrender to the guru,' he believes. 'There is no point in having such a student learn for a few hours in class and then let him go away to do other things far removed from music. A gurukul implies that the student live in the guru's house and follow the same lifestyle as the master.'

Such a gurukul where students would surrender themselves to learning with a dedication similar to the one he followed in his youth needs space. And he has no idea where he can find any in the crowded, high-priced city that he has made his home decades ago.

Once again, serendipity opens the way. The year is 1988. He gets an invitation from Rajiv Gandhi to accompany his Festival of India entourage to Japan. He is one of the eighty-member troupe that includes a sizeable team of support staff and a few artistes. They travel in a 747 Jumbo Jet which can seat 400. There is ample opportunity to have a private moment with the young prime minister. Hariprasad uses the chance to mention his dream of a gurukul. Gandhi is quick to respond, offering him 20 to 24 acres in the new developing zone that would later be known simply as Noida. The idea does not please Hariprasad who prefers to stay in Bombay, where he has established himself and where he now feels at home.

He has to be satisfied with an assurance that his wish will be entertained. But Gandhi is as good as his word.

'He phoned Sharad Pawar and told him, "Show him a few places," and that was that.'

Not long after that, the plot for the proposed gurukul is decided on. It is about 800 sq. yards, and in a posh extension of the well-developed Juhu Scheme. He is told that he must develop it and build on it within three to four years, otherwise it will be taken back. 'We had no money to build, so the place lay vacant and overgrown for ten years,' Hariprasad remembers. 'Luckily,' he adds, 'no one remembered to take it back.'

Opportunity would present itself again in the guise of a ceremony. Hariprasad is in Delhi. He has been named as worthy of a Padma Vibhushan at the Republic Day celebrations, and when the time comes to receive the honour in person, he is flown to Delhi. Alongside him, at the Rashtrapati Bhavan where they will meet the then President of India, K.R. Narayanan, is iconic industrialist and philanthropist Ratan Tata. The two awardees greet each other and spend some time exchanging news. Tata has heard Hariprasad play, and is aware of his dedication and immense contribution to Indian music. Quick to realize that the flautist is mentally preoccupied with something, he asks Hariprasad why he looks worried.

Once again, the maestro unravels the dream of a gurukul, telling Tata of his predicament. The land gifted to him stands vacant and waiting. 'Send me a proposal,' Tata says briefly. He has set the ball rolling.

'Within seven days of the proposal being dispatched, I received a letter from him, sanctioning 4 crore rupees,' Hariprasad remembers. 'The letter told me I should start work. I thought, how is this so easy . . . I felt I was dreaming!'

More was to follow. Knowing that building structures was not in the gamut of his skills and would eat into his creative time, he recalls, 'The Tatas entrusted the job to Tata Constructions. I was told, "Do not come this side, even to look. We will let you know when it is ready." Within a year, they were ready with the building . . . a kitchen, a hall for programmes, one for classes, separate bathrooms and six rooms for students, and a separate wing for me to stay. When they handed me the key, everything was ready and waiting to be occupied. I think it was one of the happiest moments in my life.'

In 2002, Hariprasad would don the mantle of a full-time guru. He would continue to travel for performances and shows across the world and his own country, but when in Bombay, his home would now be with his students, in the gurukul.

When Anuradha asks him why he is shifting out of their own home to the gurukul, his response is rooted in both logic and emotion. 'The children who live at the gurukul leave their homes, their families, loved ones to live there alone. I need to be with them, among them,' he explains simply. 'It took her a long time to understand that,' he adds.

Yet, Hariprasad is not cut off from his family. In fact, his role as a teacher started much before the Vrindaban Gurukul became a reality.

As early as 1970, Rupak Kulkarni, son of a musician, Malhar Rao Kulkarni, would sit with Hariprasad to learn to play the flute. 'He was dedicated, and I remember he played with me during *Mera Naam Joker*,' Hariprasad says. Today, Rupak has many awards and records to his credit, and is often at the gurukuls, essaying the role of a teacher.

Then there is Hariprasad's own nephew, Rakesh.

'I call him Babu-ji, and my father, Uncle, because I spent so much time with him as a kid,' says Rakesh Chaurasia, Hariprasad's younger brother's son. An established flautist himself, Rakesh had no problems adopting the instrument as his vocation. His uncle had blazed a trail he could easily follow. In the mid-1970s, Rakesh says, he started his journey as a flautist, quite casually. 'I would play with my dinky car while he was practising. And I think the sound seeped into my consciousness. One day, on his son Rajeev's birthday, he suddenly said, "Does anyone want to learn the flute?" Like a good schoolboy, I quickly put my hand up, while the others were still wondering if they wanted to respond or not. Within no time, he produced a small flute and handed it to me. I looked at the bamboo, I did not know what it was called, but I held it to my mouth and blew into it. Surprisingly, it sang. I did not know it then, but not everybody can make a flute sing the first time they blow through it. Anuradha-ji, my aunt, immediately said, "Arrey, he played it, he should learn the flute."'

Seeing his nephew constantly occupied with his new toy, blowing into it and trying to imitate sounds he heard from the radio, Hariprasad decided to teach him. 'One day, he said, "This won't do, sit down and learn properly."'

By then, Hariprasad's role as a teacher had started in earnest. A clutch of students, chosen with the master's expert eye, which, like a jeweller's keen eye, sees talent at one glance and can gauge which aspirant will combine dedication with his gift, would gather to learn from the maestro. Rakesh recalls how he would sit, 'at the back of the class that he took on Sundays, my fingers restless, my mind repeating the question, *when will I play?* My hands were still too small, I could not reach the longer flute. He had taught me the sargam, but nothing more, and I was impatient. Then, for five minutes towards the end of the class, he would write out some notes and tell me to practise . . . it would be the same routine every Sunday.'

By the time Rakesh started his Sunday classes, Hariprasad had 'become a star. He was seldom in town, or even in the country. I had to learn by listening.'

Even today, Hariprasad believes listening is the best way to learn. After all, he did learn much of his art by listening to a variety of recordings in the library at AIR Cuttack. Listening includes what others are playing in class, what teachers play and what happens when there is a stage performance. Conducting oneself on stage, handling co-artistes, audience, are all lessons learnt by watching and paying heed.

Like many of his students today, Rakesh too accompanied his uncle on a tour. 'I must have been fifteen, when he asked me if I wanted to accompany him to Russia for the Festival of India celebrations there. I jumped at the idea. He handed me the tanpura and made me play it through the first few concerts. Then one evening, he asked if I wanted to play on stage. I said yes, of course. The trips continued over the years. If he wanted me to go with him, he would ask, "Do you have exams?" and I would say no at once, letting go of an exam, if there was one imminent, for the chance to tour with him and be on stage with him. It was a great pleasure being with him; his positivity was infectious, he never says no. Listening to him sharing experiences, I learned so much. Even now, once he starts talking, I never want to get up. Most of my learning came from watching and listening to him on stage. How he presents a raga, how he checks the response of the audience and finds ways to surprise them, keep them enthralled. Every one of his students learns the same way, it is as valuable a source of knowledge as formal lessons.'

Other lessons come from just being with his uncle. 'He loves his paan, it is possibly his only weakness. On one of our trips, he was slicing supari with the sharp instrument used for the purpose, and he sliced through his thumb. He must have calmly taken out some chuna from the little box he carries along, for adding to the paan, and applied it to the wound. The chuna staunched the flow. I saw something white on his thumb when he sat down to play, but could not make out what it was. But as he started playing, the blood started pulsing out. It stained his kurta, and flowed quite freely, but he paid no heed, just kept playing till the concert was over. When we fussed over him later, he only said, "*Haan thoda sa ho gaya.*" It's just a little thing. I think it proved to me what a cool guru he is.'

Even after the establishment of the Vrindaban Gurukul, the travelling continued. Hariprasad would often take a student along to accompany him. When he was in the city, Hariprasad would guide his students, along with other teachers appointed from among his older students. In his absence, the gurukul was run by proxy, ensuring everything ran just as it did when he was in residence. There were no strict timings for classes; the rule was to be immersed in riyaz all through the day, either playing or thinking of the music. And of course, there were housekeeping duties in the manner of all gurukuls since ancient times, with students taking turns cooking, cleaning, tending to gardening and other duties. Day scholars were also admitted but were expected to be as dedicated and show steady progress through practice as the residential disciples.

'He teaches by throwing challenges to his students,' Rakesh says. He remembers one such. 'I was about six years old. The programme head of a Doordarshan children's programme called *Santakukdi* was looking for a child who could perform a short number, and Uncle simply said, "Take him", pointing to me. I was told I had to play. He taught me a fifteen-minute dhun, giving me his complete, single-minded attention for the first time. I was so happy. He got a kurta made for me to wear. I told all my school mates at my school that I was going to be on TV.'

Time would prove that Hariprasad indeed had a discerning eye. Rakesh Chaurasia would, by the age of nine, play solo for forty-five minutes at St Xavier's College. 'It was completely classical,' he recalls. 'I was under the spell of the music. And realized it got me respect from people of all levels and ages. This fact had first dawned on me during a school function. When the audience was still around and the plays had all finished, I went up to the stage saying I would play. I was a naughty boy, so the teachers were sure I was planning some new mischief. But I took my flute out and played. I could see how their attitude changed. It gave me a new seriousness. And since then, my uncle too took me more seriously.'

Perhaps realizing that he was veering more towards playing classical music, and as the demands for his performances increased, Hariprasad introduced Rakesh to the film world. 'One day, around 1987, he asked me if I wanted to play for films, and when I said I did, he took me to Pyarelal-ji. Soon I was playing in group ensembles. Then the solos came . . . *Khilaf, Khalnayak, Mr India, Prem Granth*. I got very busy. Hari-ji was also playing, but much less, as he was travelling most of the time, performing in one place or the other. I call him "Superman . . . always in the air". But I remember how, if he was in town and he came to the studio, Pyarelal-ji would make a piece for him to play, or give him a space in the music to fill in.'

Reminiscing about the early experiences in playing for films, Rakesh talks about how his uncle would play the solos if he was present, then join the others when they sat together. 'He was way above the other instrumentalists, but that made no difference to him, he never thought in that way.' He also remembers with awe and affection the wonderman of Hindi film orchestration, Manohari Singh.

'Manohari Dada would play in sync with Hari-ji, he had a silver flute, with keys. It is next to impossible to play Indian classical phrases like meend, gamak, on it, but he would be able to do it. He played the saxophone too; so beautifully, he could make it weep. Later, I was lucky to get a lot of recordings with Manohari Dada. With Hari-ji away most of the time, I was a willing substitute. At some point in class, I realized he was not happy about the quality of my playing; perhaps he felt something was lacking. I realized I needed more practice; the recordings were eating into my growth as a classical musician. I asked him, "Should I lessen my recordings, so I can practise more?" He said, "When you get work, never refuse it. If people give you respect, call you with love, go. Sleep less." I know he used to do that, work till 2 a.m. and sleep till 4, and get up again to start work. I realized I had to give up one thing . . . sleep.'

Hariprasad has often stated that he 'wants to raise a generation of musicians, like my Guruma and her father did'. Already the first generation of his students are finding their place in the world of music.

By 2010, Hariprasad had established a second gurukul, in Bhubaneswar. In a way, it was a return gift to the state that had set him on his first real journey into classical music. The second Vrindaban Gurukul is located inconspicuously in a bylane not far from the Jain caves of Udayagiri which bustle with selfie-taking visitors of all ages. The buildings that house the gurukul blend in with the greenery, and the open spaces that lie between the three main structures are conducive to open-air practice. Visitors to the gurukul may hear the rising notes of a flute played by a student practising under a tree. Sometimes, two notes mingle in the air, as individuals pursue their riyaz at different spots on the campus. At such times, the resident peacocks tend to fan out their multi-coloured tails and dance, ignoring and unafraid of the dogs of various sizes that sleep around, lulled by the sound.

Launched with much fanfare at a ceremony that had Naveen Patnaik, chief minister of Orissa, Pt Shivkumar Sharma, and Amitabh and Jaya Bachchan attending the inauguration, the gurukul that took three years to be set up now has eight rooms for students, besides a hall for classes and practice, a dining hall and kitchen, a reception area, and a two-storeyed building where Hariprasad occupies the first floor when he is in residence, while the rest of the family uses the lower section. An open-air amphitheatre provides space for in-house performances, practice and impromptu learning sessions.

The fact that the student rooms are called Shanti Nivas, the classroom is Sadhanalaya, the dining section is Annapurna, and Hari-ji and his family stay in Hari Kutir when they visit, bears testimony to the tenor of the place and the mood it seeks to create in resident and visitor alike.

The same rules apply in both gurukuls. Students are taken on purely on the basis of merit and the seriousness they show towards learning. They are housed in twin sharing rooms. Most long-term students are expected to stay and learn for five years. They pay a security deposit at the time of joining. Some students are also allowed on a month-to-month basis, to accommodate foreigners or returning students who wish to reconnect.

Hariprasad prefers to take on residential students who have some knowledge about playing on the flute, and who have studied enough to hold a basic degree.

Digvijay Singh cites himself as an example of a student of Vrindaban Gurukul. 'I learnt a bit at the Bombay gurukul in 2010–2012. It acquainted me with the art of playing the flute. I was studying for B.Tech in Ahmedabad and would shuttle between my lessons in college and class at the gurukul. Class consisted of a two-hour lesson from a senior student of Guruji. I was then expected to practise the lesson for the next two or three weeks, and return on the next holiday.'

By 2013, when his studies were completed, Digvijay knew he wanted to delve deeper into music. He shifted to Bhubaneswar and joined the gurukul as a student. 'I told Guruji I wanted to continue my studies, and he gave me the go-ahead. He believes art and education must go hand in hand. So I completed my M.Tech and am now pursuing my PhD. My formal studies feed my need to increase my knowledge. But my goal is to be a performing artiste.'

Life at the gurukul has a basic structure. Once breakfast is taken care of by 9 a.m., class begins by 10 a.m. When teachers are in residence, class goes on till 1 p.m. Otherwise, students are expected to use the time to practise. They will gather for lunch at 1 p.m., and some of them would have participated in kitchen duties. Post-lunch, the free time available can be used for rest or riyaz, depending on the need of each student, but at 4 p.m., they will gather for a class that goes on till 7 in the evening. Volunteer students on cleaning duty will spend an hour cleaning the premises before joining class. Cooking for dinner will engage two or three students by rotation, every evening at 8 p.m., and dinner is served between 9 and 10. Dinner is also the time the conversation will revolve around doubts students have encountered in their lessons, or other aspects of music. Often, after dinner, students will seek out spaces where they can continue their practice.

While there are resident teachers in the gurukuls, who take classes for day scholars as well as boarders, senior students who are on performing tours often drop in to spend a few days teaching, exchanging musical notes and guiding the students. Hariprasad, despite his globe-hopping schedules, manages to visit both gurukuls, averaging at least once in two months at Bhubaneswar, and staying on for long stretches in the Bombay gurukul.

The teachers who come by rotation to share their knowledge with the students use the same technique Hariprasad had used when he taught them.

To begin with, a student has to be taught how to sit, so he or she can handle the flute comfortably. The next step is to learn how to blow on the flute, which sounds easier than it is. While short bursts are easy, holding a note for a sustained period with the same intensity and depth of sound is necessarily something that comes only with having mastered technique and much practice.

Once the student masters the technique of playing sustained notes, the alankar lesson begins. Digvijay remembers the early steps of his own journey. 'This is the toughest; it needs plenty of work over almost two years. Learning to play the half notes is the toughest part. Almost a year-and-a-half goes in learning the full notes and to go up and down the scale, before work begins on mastering the half notes. Of course, as in most music teaching, Yaman and Bhoop are the first ragas taught. Though there is a ma+ in Yaman, it is easy as it just needs the hole to be left fully open.'

Explaining the intricacies of flute playing, Digvijay says that to play sa, pa and sa, the flautist must close the first three of the six holes in the flute for the lower sa, close all for pa, and close the first three holes again for the higher sa, but this time blow into the flute differently. Adding, 'Unlike other instruments where we need to change strings to change the scale, we need to use breath to make the change. And we can play only two octaves on the flute . . . from sa to pa in the upper scale. To go above that needs a lot of knowledge.'

Following the technique that Annapurna Devi taught her keen pupil, the students of the gurukul also learn to play the alaap in the dhrupad style.

Digvijay explains the foundations of the learning. 'Hari-ji realized that the dhrupad style allowed the listener to enter the complete mood of the raga; he could create a meditative state with his playing and draw the listener into it. The melody would wind into the listener's mind, and keep him captivated. But once the mood was created, he realized there was no need to continue in the same slow way that the dhrupad followed. It would not hold the modern listener for much longer. So he would jump into the bandish with the tabla in *madhya laya*, or medium speed. The jump would surprise and captivate the listener who would find the rhythm invigorating, and thus easily lead him to the next span of listening.

'Mixing dhrupad and khayal was Guruji's idea. He added the dhrupad style for the first time to the flute-playing technique and combined what other instrumentalists were doing in playing jod and jhala to take the tempo into more exciting areas that most listeners found fascinating in the sitar, for example. Besides this, he would take the range of taals beyond the teen taal and roopak taal, which were the taals usually played in madhya laya. His innovations include the eleven-matra taal, pancham sawari taal . . . unusual taals not used by instrumentalists and even more rarely by singers. In fact, Guruji created a musical presentation style all his own, as any music connoisseur knows.'

Digvijay Singh goes on, 'When he moves to drut, the faster tempo, he would use tantra work, like that used by string instruments, to delineate the music. He would incorporate taan styles from various gharanas, adding the style of the vocalist, blending in Western music techniques, gamaks, sapat taan, or the danedar style. It is not easy to do this in the flute, but he blends it all effortlessly, seamlessly, and explores the raga. He takes the best from classical and semi-classical forms, elements from the thumri, bhajan, even the bihu dance songs of Assam and folk music, and can play them all. In fact,' Digvijay adds, his eyes shining with enthusiasm as he tries to convey what he has observed of his guru's mastery over his medium, 'he is able to create *bhav* in a thumri without the use of words.'

Besides creating a style uniquely his own, Hariprasad is also credited with creating a clutch of new ragas, which include the Shivanjali, the Indira Kalyan in honour of Indira Gandhi, and a complex amalgamation of many ragas which he named Manaranjani.

As much to be sure that his students learn to understand and explore music for themselves as to encourage them to continue their involvement with music, Hariprasad has evolved a teaching method very different from most classical gurus.

'He gives us three surs to work on. Tells us to take them back and use them to improvise.' Digvijay tries to explain the mentor's unique method of teaching. 'So we could have pa-sa-pa or pa-dha-sa, and we have to improvise and find ways to express with these three notes. Then one more note would be added, pa-dha-sa-re, and we start again, finding new combinations, trying to understand the feelings they evoke.

'Learning gamak, meend, and other such ornamentations and asking us to add them to the improvisations was his way of teaching technique. Then the sound is never the same even if a phrase is repeated.

'Students are also taught to start with a long note to improve lung capacity. Holding a note for up to thirty seconds is not easy, but we try to get there. The notes also have to be in perfect sync with the tanpura; we practise till we are as close as possible. It is the way to get the sur settled in the mind, and sharpen the ears. Of course, one learns by listening to records or from books that give notations, but improvisation teaches independence and develops the individual style that is so vital a part of classical music. It is important to know each sur perfectly because breath and finger position can make a difference, and change re to komal re.'

Besides improvisation as a learning method, Hariprasad's students are encouraged to listen to music, be it folk, classical, or fusion, and to get to know their mood and nuances and the feelings they evoke.

But above all, the guru teaches his students the virtue of humility, by example. 'I accompanied him for one of his SPIC MACAY concerts, which he does regularly as one way to take music to children and students,' Digvijay recollects. 'He was playing, and I was to accompany him on the tanpura. We travelled by train. I realized on the trip how respected he is, how much respect he commands even from people who do not know him at all. He behaves with everyone in the same way, with gentleness, and there is no sign that he is a towering personality in the music field. This was new to me, and I think I realized then the extent of his greatness.

'On that trip, Hariprasad performed at Vikas Public School, where he played Yaman for the student audience, knowing the sweetness of the raga would appeal to young minds. He went on to play bhajans and even a few jingles to entertain the younger ones in the audience . . . [He had] no hang-ups about his being a classical musician who would not "stoop" to playing jingles. He was an entertainer of children and knew how to catch their interest by playing tunes they recognize. It was his way of capturing their interest in music.'

'Whenever I get a chance, I learn from him,' Rakesh Chaurasia says, adding, 'He always has something new to serve. He practises as a means of exploring and finding new ways of executing what he wants to convey. He seldom expresses his feelings in words, be it joy or sorrow; but when he plays, he expresses it all. Others may play more difficult stuff, but his passion is unique and gives his music that inimitable quality. He said to me once, "When you play, gods and goddesses sit with you, listen to you, and bless you." I realized then that, for him, playing is like being in the presence of [Goddess] Saraswati. Though he plays an instrument limited in its scope, he never feels it. He has learnt to make it do whatever he wants it to. And passes it on to us. We are lucky, we get it readymade.'

An Interlude

Pt Hariprasad Chaurasia is performing at a concert in Dhaka. He has been visiting the city every year for an annual performance where his fans and music lovers throng to listen to the melody of his flute. He does not know it, but in the audience is a young woman whose life he has influenced considerably. She is a student of the piano, and holds a job as a public health researcher.

As a youngster, even as she learnt to play the piano, she would also play the flute, casually. The flute is a handy, portable instrument, and so when she left home to study in the US for her master's degree, she decided to carry her flute with her as a way of keeping in touch with music. When she found a teacher who could help her play the instrument better, she acquainted herself with ragas, over 'on-and-off' classes that spanned four years.

Then, at the concert, as she listens to Hariprasad Chaurasia playing, she comes to a decision. She will find a place among his students. He would be her guru.

Without a qualm or a second thought, she quits her job, allays her parents' fears, and makes the necessary phone calls to confirm that she can fly to Bhubaneswar.

Musarrat Jabeen Rahman has been in the gurukul in Bhubaneswar now for two years. She accompanies Hariprasad to Dhaka when he goes there on his annual visit.

'She is a good student,' affirms the maestro, who makes it a point to meet Musarrat's mother in Dhaka on every visit to reassure her of her daughter's safety and progress.

When Musarrat landed at the gurukul, she recollects, 'My first thought was, this is a resort! The vibe is so beautiful.'

She was impressed by the fact that everybody had to play in class, and share skills as well as mistakes, so each of the others could learn what to adopt and what to avoid. Thanks to practice on the flute over the years, 'My fingers were flexible, but I found improvisation very tough. I still struggle with it. I am working on three ragas—Bhairav, Ahir Bhairav and Lalit. But, of course, how many ragas you know is not the important thing. What matters to Guruji is how well you familiarize yourself with them. Because then you can challenge yourself . . . and if you hear a new raga, see how fast you can pick it up.'

Despite the struggle of improvisation and her reticence in playing in front of others, Musarrat is determined to continue. 'I changed my flute for an Indian one and recently got a full set,' she says. 'I do not plan to give up so easily.'

Hariprasad's own views on improvisation besides being logical give an insight into the uniqueness of his style of playing.

He believes, 'Improvisation is a way of making anything beautiful. Take paper. It can be used for creating a painting, or making a paper flower, or a book . . . [It's] the same with a bandish, or poetry. It forms the base; one has to decorate it, but without moving away from the raga. Then the best way to do it is to keep three notes and develop on them, see how to embellish them to create new sounds. Adding rhythm adds further beauty.'

He goes on to elaborate: 'The fun with improvisation is that each person is different; some will use rhythm, others will dwell on the sound and create long notes. And it will change with time, environment, audience and raga. For example, one cannot start on *laykaari* in a temple where sadhus are sitting; the music must suit the occasion and a full grasp is necessary to be able to adapt. Improvisation teaches this.'

He has mastered the art of blending myriad styles. 'I have learnt to blend styles of dhrupad, singers, instruments. To take the best from each gharana I listen to and make it my own. To wonder, if I use pakhavaj, what will happen. So I sat with Arjun Sejwal, a pakhavaj player, and asked him, "How do you do dhrupad jod?" Then I used it in jod, and it added a new dimension to my playing, because it gave it weight. The flute is an instrument that can be played by itself, without rhythm. But adding rhythm adds a new joy. Other times, I have used the ghatam or the mridangam . . . a vocabulary is created in this way. It makes it more interesting for students too. However, music must be beautiful, simple enough to appeal to a child.'

A simple explanation for the amazing dexterity with which Hariprasad is able to create intricate and astounding jugalbandi partnerships with other musicians who have also mastered their art—be it Kishori Amonkar, Pandit Jasraj, Balamuralikrishna or T.N. Krishnan, John McLaughlin or Ian Anderson—and to create magical team-ups with any instrumentalist.

In the Ramayana, when Ram goes into exile, his brother, Bharat, is designated as the king of the land, in accordance with the wishes of his mother, Kaikeyi, who has deviously ensured her son supersedes his eldest stepbrother.

Bharat, who loves his brothers and has utmost filial respect for Ram, does not accept the throne. Instead, he places his brother's footwear, or *paduka*, on the throne and rules by proxy, all the while awaiting Ram's return to take his rightful place as ruler once the period of exile is over.

In modern-day Rotterdam, a French musician, Henri Tournier, is emulating Bharat's example. In the months of the year when his guru, Hariprasad Chaurasia, is not in residence at the Music Conservatory, Tournier, his able assistant, makes sure the students have access to the guru's teachings by proxy. *Hariprasad Chaurasia and the Art of Improvisation* is Tournier's version of his guru's paduka. A hardbound volume that symbolizes the instrument it celebrates and teaches about classical music, the book includes paintings by artist Sujata Bajaj as well as CDs of Hariprasad's recitals on ragas, as additions to the text.

Tournier makes the concept of Hindustani classical music understandable even to lay readers of the book by writing about the oral tradition that characterizes it, the adaptation of the system to the teaching of Western students, and the uniqueness of the art of improvisation as conceptualized by Hariprasad as a method of teaching.

To quote from the introductory section on improvisation:

> At the end of one of my study trips in India seventeen years ago, Hariprasad Chaurasia told me about his project to join the Rotterdam Conservatory. He then offered me the chance of assisting him, so that I continue to follow his teaching. This was the starting point of a fascinating educational adventure that has completely changed my vision of music and teaching.
>
> Necessity is the mother of invention: Every year Hariprasad spends a few months in Rotterdam. Due to this, he has always generously allowed students to record sessions. Therefore, with the passing years, Hariprasad Chaurasia, trusting me as a translator and a 'go-between', rather than writing a few lines of improvisation at the end of a session as an aid to memory, has started to record tailor-made improvisations for each student. These recordings, real brief concert pieces adapted to the level and abilities of the students, in addition to traditional teaching, have become one of our teaching materials.

Explaining the use of the recorded material, Tournier goes on to write:

> Students first listen and learn, and then I help them transcribe the recording in Indian notation. A third, intermediate step consists of working on this transcript like a study with the help of the audio file, not to become its performer, but to try and feel the meaning from the inside, by playing it . . . The ultimate goal is just to use this teaching material as a framework, and a generative point of reference for the work of improvisation.

An Interlude

He is on a concert tour in Japan, and the phone in his hotel room rings. To his surprise, it is not the usual courtesy call from the hotel reception asking if all is fine and whether he is comfortable. The voice at the other end explains that he is sorry to disturb Hariprasad in Japan, but it has been very tough to track him down during his incessant travels, and since he has finally got him on the phone, he finds it necessary to pass on an important message to him. Hariprasad listens in disbelief as he learns that he is being invited by no less a personage than Queen Beatrix of Holland, to play for her. He has also been made aware that the recital is a present on the Queen's birthday from her husband, Prince Claus. When he puts down the phone, his face is flushed. As much by the honour the invitation has conferred upon him as by the fact that he has agreed. He takes a long breath. When his mind alerts him to the fact that the on-demand concert is 'next week', he finds the need to sit down on the nearest chair.

Once the moment of confusion clears, Hariprasad sets about ensuring that he will honour the commitment he has just made. A series of quick phone calls later, he has assurances that Zakir Hussain will fly down from America to play on the tabla, and his student, Rupak Kulkarni, will fly in from India to provide secondary support.

The recital, which has the performers winging in from different parts of the world, creates history. Hariprasad is the first Indian to play at the royal palace in The Hague!

The performance would have far-reaching effects. By being broadcast live across the country by a local TV station, Hariprasad's flute reaches many homes. Not surprisingly, it captivates the minds of countless listeners.

The title 'Officer in the Order of Orange-Nassau' is bestowed upon Hariprasad by the royal family on his seventieth birthday, in 2008.

'My teaching stint at Rotterdam Conservatory came out of nowhere,' the venerated artiste says, as he recounts how another phone call started him off on this new journey as a teacher, much before he could establish his gurukuls.

He was in London at that time. Joep Bor and John Floore, the two gentlemen who called to check if they could meet him, were from Rotterdam. John was the director of the Rotterdam Conservatory, where music and dance were offered as specialized disciplines, and Joep Bor was the head of the World Music Department. Both men were accomplished musicians themselves. Floore played the trumpet in the Rotterdam Philharmonic Orchestra and Bor was a trained sarangi player who had learnt from India's leading sarangi exponent, Pandit Ram Narayan, besides learning vocal singing from other Indian maestros. Bor wanted to add Hariprasad to the list of teachers of various musical traditions from across the world, as the teacher of Indian classical music.

As this was no royal request, Hariprasad could think it over. He would eventually agree to take up the offer, and set aside four months of the year, from March to June, to teach at the conservatory. He also made arrangements to make it possible for him to accept invitations to perform even during the four months at the conservatory. The simple reason being, 'I had to support my family, and it was also important to stay in the musical circle.' He also decided he would request Henri Tournier to be his assistant at the conservatory.

The stint at the Rotterdam Conservatory started in 1991 and continues to this day, although he missed going in 2019. His students come from all over the world. Despite the World Music section, including the vocal, percussion and other instruments, it is the flute section that has the most enrolments. Hariprasad believes that the serious students number fifteen or so in every batch, across disciplines of music.

A blog by Jan Reichow, reproduced here from the website *India Instruments*, titled 'Homage to his 75th Birthday', perhaps helps to explain what makes the flute one of the most popular courses at the conservatory and his playing so loved the world over:

But how was the veritable triumph of the gentle bansuri flute in the West possible, 20 years after the 'sitar explosion' (quote from Ravi Shankar). Probably because it was catchy even to people who, otherwise, had difficulties opening up to alien music. In addition, the artist got a lot of attention for some very successful experiments in fusion music. The common amalgam came from tabla wizard Zakir Hussain, who was also involved in Cologne in 1985, but had already stirred crowds in the '70s with the band Shakti. In 1986, he recorded the album *Making Music* together with Hariprasad Chaurasia, John McLaughlin and Jan Garbarek, which was received as one of the most compelling examples in the history of musical East-West meetings. The word "bansuri" became a household name. Whether in rhythmic jazz or in silent meditation centres—where the bansuri was sometimes explicitly required solo, without the nuisance tabla!—everybody loved the Indian flute with its blend of virtuosity and mellifluousness. And yet, this artist never lost his credibility for grand traditional raga presentations, with his great development in classical purity and with stunning accuracy. I'll never forget that it was his interpretation of the Raga Lalit which inspired me when I was looking for an Indian counterpart to Mozart—especially for the sensual ambivalence, as it unfolds in the opera *Cosi fan tutte*. Was it not the same phenomenon that is shown in Raga Lalit? And no one expressed surprise when the classical music station WDR3 presented about 30 minutes of Indian music in the afternoon, changing back and forth between Mozart and Raga Lalit—one experienced first-hand that both musical worlds are supported by the same spirit.

In fact, the West could not but be impressed when they attended a recital by Hariprasad. His simple manner and obvious humility, along with the magic of his playing during which he seemed almost to be elsewhere, in another dimension, communicated his sacred involvement with his art. It was an attitude that would change even the students at the conservatory, who started absorbing the link between Indian music and the divine, and treating their learning and their instruments as tools of worship.

This is what Hariprasad told a German journalist who interviewed him for a WDR programme some years ago: 'I just sit there, I am mute, holding a piece of bamboo in my hands, but someone plays it and someone listens, and there's someone between the audience and me, too. This is, I guess, a higher force. And for this higher force I play, and if this higher force has joy in the music, we also enjoy the music, the music lovers and myself.'

Hariprasad has, by example, instilled the concept of bhakti in a cross section of students, many of whom might even be atheists. And the divinity they bow before is music.

Greek mythology attributes the invention of the flute to Athena. The story is that she played on it, until she chanced to look into a mirror while playing it and saw how blowing it puffed up her cheeks and distorted her face. She abandoned the instrument immediately, throwing it away, never to pick it up again.

Hariprasad's technique of holding the flute on the underlip and blowing into it allows for no distortion of cheeks or face. And not surprisingly, the soft call of the flute has attracted a large number of women to learn the instrument.

An Interlude

The Nehru Centre auditorium in Bombay is full, the audience has gathered to listen to flute recitals played by his students to celebrate Hariprasad's seventieth birthday. One by one, the students take their place on stage and play their tribute. Among them is a pretty, young girl in a resplendent silk sari, wearing a bindi, and bedecked with light ornaments.

The audience, which includes Amitabh and Jaya Bachchan, Shivkumar Sharma and his wife, Manorama, singer Sonu Nigam, Anup Jalota, and many other well-wishers, is enthralled by the player's mastery over her instrument. The solo recital over, she takes her guru's blessings as she leaves the stage.

Later, intrigued by the player's virtuosity, Amitabh Bachchan asks Hariprasad which state the girl belongs to. Her manner of dress and conduct is reminiscent of an earlier generation. To the actor's surprise, Hariprasad tells him, she is not an Indian. She lives in Bonn, Germany, and is a student at the Rotterdam Conservatory.

'Indeed, she is one of my most dedicated students,' the master flautist says of Stephanie Bosch, the girl who captivated Bachchan with her skilful performance.

'When I heard him for the first time, I knew this was the sound I was looking for,' Stephanie says in an email interview.

Stephanie heard Hariprasad's flute while at the Rotterdam Conservatory. 'I had free time and went to the library where you could listen to all kinds of music from all over the globe. When I picked [up] and listened to one of Guruji's CDs—Raga Malkauns I remember—I was blown away. I got goosebumps and felt that was the sound I seemed to be searching for . . . At that time, I had not even heard or had contact with Indian music, and from the CD, it was not immediately obvious where this music comes from. I asked someone next to me if he had ever listened to it and he answered that Hariprasad Chaurasia is one of the teachers at that school. Then I remembered I had seen him once. And then I tried to just meet him. I had to wait three months! When I met him, he was surrounded by around eight to ten students in a very tiny room, all sitting on the floor. That was strange for me at that time.'

Finally, Stephanie was admitted to the class. Hariprasad welcomed her into the fold of students. 'Guruji was very welcoming and someone gave me a flute to join. Oh, it was far too big for me and I rejected it. Then they said I should take it home. When I was alone with the flute, my journey started . . .'

Although Stephanie had played the Western flute or 'recorder' ever since she was a child, 'and even learnt to play the transverse flute, a handmade wooden one, and even the silver flute,' she found the Indian flute a challenge.

'I can say it was difficult for me to put my small fingers on the big flute and I suffered a lot. Now my body has got adjusted to it and I feel comfortable. Learning Indian music requires a totally different approach than what I was used to, but Guruji picks every student from where he or she comes from. You need a lot of resilience to continue playing as you keep learning all the time, as with any instrument. Your body and mind get in tune with the instrument and the music, as later on the journey, the music plays itself or, as you can say, you become the instrument,' Stephanie says of her journey to mastering the instrument.

Soon, the young German was driving for three hours from Bonn, where she lived, for a one-hour class with her guru. Sometimes, she was part of a group of other students who took his classes, but mostly she was taught individually. And then soon, 'I did my first small performance at school.'

Since that start in 1998, Stephanie 'met Guruji in the Netherlands every spring for a couple of months, then again in winter and in India as well. I finished my master's in 2007; it feels as if it was yesterday. Since then I regularly meet Guruji every year; though he joked with me and said, after my exams I would not come and see him . . . but after my exams, we were diving very deep into the music as there was no time pressure any more and we spent such beautiful times with deep music and talk about music. Learning Indian classical music is a full surrender to it. Then you can make it and you enjoy it. As you start diving deeper, the more joy comes.'

As is the case with many other students at the gurukul, Stephanie's happiest moments as a performer are when she is performing with Guruji. 'Playing with Guruji on stage is something different. You feel very close and dive together into the music. We learn so much by accompanying him on stage. I remember, for example, in the beginning, when he gave me space to play, but [it] seemed I was not ready yet to play in that moment, on the spot. So I learned from that day to be prepared at any time. I now teach my students the same thing . . . We learn to be sensitive to feel when, if, how and how much we should play to give him good support.

'I have a beautiful memory of a concert in Italy with him. We played Hemavati. It was wonderful. Another time, we played Madhuvanti and Yaman and a few other ragas. He gave me a lot of space to discover and improvise, and I never forget his happy face and smile afterwards.'

'Most Indian classical musicians restrict passing on their knowledge to anyone outside their immediate family, but he teaches anyone who reaches out to him, if he finds they have the aptitude and ability to learn,' says Anuradha Chaurasia, talking about what sets her husband apart as a teacher. Over the years, 'I have noticed the generous love he gives to his students, not holding back anything as he teaches them. I don't think he gives his family the same degree of love. Though he is very dutiful as a family man, and thinks far ahead for all of us, including his granddaughters.'

Perhaps, this unique openness comes from Hariprasad's own journey as a student, where he found teachers ready to lead him one step ahead, despite his complete lack of musical credentials or antecedents. It is also the reason that the flautist can boast of students in practically every part of the globe. During his years as a classical performer, he has had institutions dedicated to him in the role of a teacher.

Surjit Singh mentions the Vrindaban Academy of Indian Classical Music and Dance started in 1992 in Hong Kong, and inaugurated on 10 October 1992 with a concert by Hariprasad in a hall that seated 2000. Singh states it was the 'first-ever concert at the venue by an Indian classical musician'. The academy would invite other top-notch artistes, including Pt Jasraj, Pt Shivkumar Sharma, Pt Hridaynath Mangeshkar, Guru Kelucharan Mohapatra, among others, on a regular basis, as a fundraiser to supplement the earnings from fees. Singh adds that it was at one such concert that, after listening to Hariprasad's solo recital, M. Balamuralikrishna, who was also there at the academy to perform, came up with the now famous statement, 'My name is Balamuralikrishna, but you can call me Krishna, because he has taken away my flute.'

Hariprasad would visit the academy about twice a year, and 'hold informal sessions with the students'. He would also address students and hold lecture demonstrations at the music departments of the Chinese University of Hong Kong, and other universities around, almost till the academy closed down in the year 2000.

Not wishing to disappoint any lover of the flute who wishes to learn from him, Hariprasad makes it a point to combine a visit to Italy every time he goes to Rotterdam. He laughs with childlike happiness as he describes his visits there.

'I go to Italy every year after my stint in Holland; my friend, Lorenzo, teaches flute at the conservatory in Vicenza. Lorenzo organizes a master class for me. Afterwards, we spend three days in a village near Milan . . . Italian wine, pasta, cheese . . . Italian food is so different. We all stay together, it is wonderful.'

'Always in the Air'

It is very difficult to keep track of Hariprasad's whereabouts. Over the years, his schedule has included frequent travels for performances across the world, in countries as far flung as Sweden and China, where local audiences have responded thunderously to Indian classical music as rendered through the humble flute.

His concerts, often solo, at other times with other internationally known musicians, including Egberto Gismonti, John McLaughlin and Ian Garbarek, are the stuff of legend.

He has played in Seoul, where he teamed up with a Korean flute player named Jang-Hyun Won, and with the legendary Ian Anderson of Jethro Tull in Dubai—both memorable concerts that displayed Hariprasad's ability to adapt to any music, without compromising his own.

The Seoul performance, in 1993, was notable, because after listening to Jang-Hyun Won demonstrating a Korean folk tune to him at dinner the previous evening, Hariprasad wowed the audience by reproducing it from memory, before starting on his own recital.

Perhaps nothing speaks more eloquently of his globetrotting than the fact that, on the evening, almost immediately after his son's wedding reception, on 3 January 1997, Hariprasad was rushing to catch a plane to Paris.

'He still likes to say yes to everyone, and thinks nothing of flying from Bombay to Benaras and, from there, the next morning to Kerala,' says Pushpanjali, who also goes by the name of Kasturi.

Hariprasad's daughter-in-law is now his manager, taking on the duties of accepting shows, and ascertaining that he has no worries about flights and other such mundanities.

'Papa managed it all himself earlier,' she says, adding that his modus operandi was to leave the house for the airport for early-morning international flights without disturbing anyone in the house. 'Mummy would leave something for him to eat on the dining table, and he would eat and leave. He would handle all the phone calls and faxes that precede a show himself. His memory holds phone numbers like a phone book; he can reel off any number without batting an eyelid.' And when the family travelled, 'He would take charge of all the passports, and tickets, knew what visas had been got, payments made . . . it was mindblowing!'

The only time Hariprasad made a mistake was in December 2018. He was eighty years old, but happily flying on his own to Rotterdam.

'We dropped Babuji off at the airport, and returned. We learnt much later what had happened. When he tried to enter the airport, the security stopped him. The photograph on his passport looked different. As a frequent traveller, he had a sheaf of passports, kept together, and he had taken the wrong one!'

Pushpanjali tells it as it happened. 'It was around 2 a.m., but he quietly turned back. He had no phone with him to call us back, he had left it behind with Rajeev. We knew nothing of what had happened. At 3.30 in the morning, the phone rang. It was Babuji on the phone, and he was saying, "I am at the gurukul, I am back. I took the wrong passport. I did not want to disturb you, so I went to the gurukul." I was shocked. But he calmly changed his flight to the next day. We were surprised when he told us the security said even Immigration would let him through, but he would certainly be stopped in France and not allowed to enter with the old passport, and they could even possibly deport him.'

Pushpanjali grew accustomed to waking up to the sound of her father-in-law's flute as he practised at dawn.

She recounts her amazement at the punishing schedule he kept without any sign of fatigue, and remembers, 'He would go from the airport from an early-morning flight straight to the BMC school, that he had been allowed to use right in the beginning, when he had started teaching Rupak Kulkarni and others. He would rest only after lunchtime.'

When she was still new at her self-appointed job as manager to Hariprasad, Pushpanjali would sometimes find herself out of her depth. 'There were times I booked him at two events on the same date or time, but he never lost his cool. Instead, he would calm me down and think on how to rectify it. When I was doing all the paperwork, he would gently remind me of possible omissions.'

Giving another example of Hariprasad's ability to stay cool and look at the positive side, Pushpanjali mentions a recital where he played at a wedding at Hyderabad's Chowmahalla Palace. 'He had agreed to play at a wedding only because a friend had requested him. But the audience seated at the function was just not interested, they were all taking selfies with each other, and it was distracting, to say the least. The tabla players were upset, they felt it was insulting, but Papa just smiled and told them, '*Practice toh ho gaya na.*' (At least practice got done.) Again, when only eight people turned up for a recital in a church in Europe, he joked saying it was a good place for a rehearsal. Of course, for me it was not as easy, I felt I had subjected him to humiliation, and berated myself for saying okay to the programme. I felt the earth should open and swallow me . . . but he said nothing to me at all.'

An Interlude

The year is 2009. Hariprasad is to perform in Rome. Once the performance is over, the next day is free with nothing scheduled till their departure for Naples. Pushpanjali decides to visit the Vatican. She notices that Hariprasad is not at breakfast, but thinks nothing much of it. When Pushpanjali boards the bus for Naples, she is surprised that Hariprasad is late. Which he never is. She goes to his room, and sees him sitting there. He looks at her and says simply, 'I want to go to the hospital.'

'Parkinson's had just started for him. I knew it was something serious.' Though Pushpanjali feels a mounting panic, Hariprasad is calm through the ride to the hospital. She waits anxiously while the doctors carry out their investigations. They discover insufficient blood is reaching his brain. Luckily, he shows a quick response to the medication administered. But when the doctors tell him they want him to stay under observation for twenty-four hours, he sits up. 'I came on my own accord, I need to leave at my will,' he says. They are helpless and can't stop him. 'He performed on schedule in Naples,' Pushpanjali says.

'He does not let anything stop him from his commitments,' Pushpanjali adds. 'When his health is down and he feels low, he says no to requests for recitals, but the moment he is better, he says, "I'll go!" He drives for hours, takes connecting flights without a second thought, and only carries hand luggage on most trips. His response to our worrying about him is, 'If something has to happen to me, it can happen anywhere.'

Although he did not follow his father and become an instrumentalist, Rajeev Chaurasia takes a constant interest in the senior's work and brings in aspects that will appeal to his generation.

According to Surjit Singh, Rajeev was instrumental in turning his father's wish to play with Ian Anderson into reality. Working over four years, the younger Chaurasia kept up the reminders, till Anderson could find a time slot for The Jethro Tull Hariprasad Chaurasia Desert Fusion Concert, their first performance, held at the Mina Seyahi Auditorium in Dubai on 29 January 2004. The two would perform again in Bombay, at the NCPA on 31 January and 1 February 2004. To quote from *Woodwinds of Change*:

Singh adds that after Hariprasad's rendition of Raga Durga and Jethro Tull's selection of music, the audience listened, enraptured, to an hour of fusion, 'consisting mainly of improvisations on a basic structure composed by Hariprasad in Raga Jog. Although each went into the other's domain, it was more like Anderson playing raga than Hariprasad playing rock . . . an approach that seemed to work for both of them.'

Recounting his performances at diverse concerts through the years can make for repetitive reading, but there were a few that bear mention due to their extraordinary nature, or because of the circumstances surrounding them.

Shyamala Rajender, a California-based attorney who has been instrumental in organizing many of Hariprasad's shows in America, has some memories to share from among them. Shyamala heard of Hariprasad through Chitti Babu, the famous veena player, 'from whom I learnt the veena for a brief period. He was a family friend. Chitti Babu told me to listen to his music and try and meet him.'

That was not to happen in the immediate future. Shyamala, like many south Indian girls who came of marriageable age in the 1960s, moved to the US when she married Rajender who was settled there. Chance found her listening to Hariprasad at a concert in New York in 1987, and she realized why Chitti Babu had made the suggestion. She was entranced by the veteran flautist's music.

A few years later, when Hariprasad was playing at San Jose, Shyamala met him. The conversation that took place between them would have a lingering impact.

Hariprasad mentioned that he toured America because it gave him a huge audience, but was quite uncomfortable with the unprofessional attitude of those who organized his tours. He looked at the visiting card Shyamala had offered, and the thought struck him that she might have the skills required to organize his tours.

'My first reaction was, "I am a biochemist and an attorney, and know only a little about music,"' she recounted during a telephone interview. 'I asked him why he thought me capable of what he was asking. But he was persuasive and would not take no for an answer. Very gently but firmly, he said, "You can do it."'

As a result of Hariprasad's persuasion, Shyamala took on the task of organizing his tours in America.

Prominent in her memories is the first concert she arranged for him. 'I told him, "Let me try one show, if it works, I will look ahead." And I started work. Ambitiously, I booked a 3500-seater hall. My initial anxiety about filling it was allayed; the hall was packed on the day of the show.'

It's been twenty years since that concert, but sharp in her memory is a concert she organized in New Mexico. 'The organizers there were nervous, concerned about the audience not even having been exposed to Indian music, and they asked me, "How will he handle it?" I told them he had an unusual way of giving the audience what they like. And then, he performed. And the audience listened in rapture as he played till 1 a.m. When he stopped, they wanted him to go on, and when he finally closed, they would not let him go, but kept talking to him, asking questions. And no, he had not compromised one bit on his music, and played only classical Indian ragas, but he had held the audience right through.'

Shyamala also arranged a gargantuan twenty-six-city tour in 2004 for the flautist. 'We toured cities on both East and West coasts. I worked out the schedule in such a way that the travel would be minimized. The programmes were arranged in each town or city by local organizers who entered into contracts through me. I ensured the journeys would not be over two to two-and-a-half hours. We travelled the road routes in a van which I drove, while longer journeys were by air. And I ensured we were given nice hotels to stay in. The tour was a huge success, as it also introduced younger talent, including Rimpa Siva whose dexterity on the tabla won rave reviews and huge applause.'

As was his wont, Hariprasad often let the younger artistes enjoy their moment on stage. Shyamala doubled up as tanpura player on the tour. Of that experience, she says, 'Actually, with some practice, even a trained monkey can play the tanpura, and I had had some practice in my younger days.' She adds that though it was initially daunting to sit with such a huge personage on the same platform, she enjoyed the experience. 'In fact, I had two tanpuras I had ordered in Delhi, from a Sanjay Sharma. They were both in E scale, which is what Hari-ji requires. I carried them along, and it saved him the trouble of bringing one over from India.'

There was also a memorable tour in Nova Scotia, at a music camp. 'Across two performances by him, we had 150 students aged between three and eighty years, hailing from across the world, attending.'

Since practically the first tour she organized for him, 'Hari-ji comes across to stay at my place. I have a big, four-bedroom house with bathrooms. I give him and his family one wing, with two bedrooms, and let him enjoy the peace. More recently, he likes to just chill, away from people. I let him relax, be himself. Sometimes, though, I take him out for a meal. Otherwise, I cook. He likes fish, and goat curry, and it is a constant request when I ask him what he would like.' Hariprasad also relishes, 'upma and dosa, which I make for him. Often, my daughter or brother, who is very fond of Hari-ji, drop in, and we have a warm family time when he is here.'

With the passing of years, there have been changes in her role. 'I stopped organizing tours in 2012 when my husband passed away. I have set up a few concerts, in 2014 and the following year, but it was in this area. I don't plan tours any more.'

Also memorable for Pushpanjali, given her own role in it, is the concert by the Shivkumar Sharma–Hariprasad Chaurasia duo with Shubhankar Banerjee on the tabla, at the Nobel Peace Awards ceremony in 1998 in Oslo, Norway. Pushpanjali was also on stage, to accompany the instrumentalists on the tanpura. Or so it seemed to the audience. But Hariprasad had planned something else altogether.

Knowing that there would be many recitals by artistes from other countries, including Elton John, Enrique Iglesias and Alanis Morissette, who were waiting in the wings, and wanting to impress the august audience gathered for such a prestigious event, he had planned to present an unforgettable thirty minutes of music.

As he started playing, he quickly moved into jhala, and signalled to Pushpanjali to sing slokas in Sanskrit at a slow pace. 'In fact, perhaps because I might be a bit nervous, he himself started reciting the shanti slokas with me, then let me continue.'

The contrast proved electric; the slow soft rhythmic recitation set against the fast tempo of the flute left an impression not easily forgotten.

An Interlude

Hariprasad is visiting James Galway, a famous Irish flautist. A narration culled from an interview at NCPA with Arvind Parikh: 'I saw he had three golden flutes. Pure 999.9 gold. He plays on it. He offers it to me, and I play on it. His flute has a mouthpiece which makes playing much easier. Of course, our flutes do not have that. I have my bamboo flute with me. I show it to him. He says, "May I play it?" I nod, of course. So he blows into the flute. And nothing happens. He cannot play it. He hands it back to me. I ask him, "Do you want to keep my flute? You can try to play it later. We can exchange flutes if you wish." He looks at me, surprised. Then says, "I only have these flutes and have many concerts. I cannot give it to you."'

He does not say in the interview whether he told Galway that he was of course joking, but tells the interviewer, 'I was thinking then, if I had got the flute, how much money I would have made from it!'

Few people know that Hariprasad created a symphony for the Birmingham Royal Ballet, UK. He explains how it came about. 'They wanted three pieces, one by a Black, one by a European, and they asked me if I would create the third. I liked the idea. It was the first time an Indian was being included in something like this. We each had thirty minutes. I took a composition titled *Krishna* that I had made earlier, and adapted it so it could be played by the Western orchestra along with my flute.'

His forays into introducing Indian classical music to the Western psyche included a workshop at Harvard, which has a musical therapy department. Hariprasad was 'invited to interact with the students, and we worked on understanding how ragas affect us, how each raga affects one differently'. Could not have been difficult for such a consummate player who evokes deep emotions through his flute.

Stories of Hariprasad's determination to play tell of true grit, and belie the soft persona of a man whose eyes twinkle as he speaks, and whose gentleness extends to all whom he encounters in his life.

The gentleness transforms into serious action when it comes to helping others, Rajeev informs me. And indeed, Hariprasad has never hesitated in calling up school authorities to get admission for a friend's child, and has gone to great lengths to find a good school for his helper's children. His pocket is often filled with sweets when he goes to his gurukul in Bhubaneswar. Unashamed to ask favours for others, he can make repeated calls to tardy officials in government or municipalities, to get his demands addressed. 'He never gives up, and he never forgets,' Pushpanjali says, of his fight for others' causes. 'He can never stay still, and handles so many things at one time; keeps everyone on their toes saying, call that person, remind this one, ask what happened. It is rare for someone of his stature to worry so actively about others, but he is like that.'

Anuradha adds that he has been relentlessly pursuing the authorities to have them give him the plot adjoining the gurukul. He says, 'Give it to me, I will beautify it, rid it of the ghodawallas and druggies who camp there, and build a beautiful Vrindavan Vatika. He chases the commissioner, the chief minister, without forgetting; when the chief minister changes, he calls whoever has occupied the chair!' she adds, laughing.

The goodwill he enjoys is immeasurable. It is rare to meet anyone not moved by his music, but it is his humane nature that shines through and makes the man much loved. Across musicians of all ages, he commands both love and respect as much for his simplicity as for his talent. 'It has been my good fortune to have been able to associate with so many great musicians. They seemed to enjoy my music and were gracious to ask me to join them. I have never felt uncomfortable with any genre. I think it is only a difference in style. It is like speaking different languages. For me, there is only one language, the language of music,' Hariprasad said in an interview to K. Prasad for the *Hindu*, on 1 February 2018. He mined the goodwill when, in the mid-1980s, Anuradha was making *Sadhana*, a television series on the musical greats of India, that was aired on Doordarshan.

One of Anuradha's memories of *Sadhana* is that both the Mangeshkar sisters were part of it. 'I went to Lata-ji and told her the concept of the serial and she immediately offered to be a part of the episode on Ustad Bismillah Khan. We shot in this house, Savitri, and she sat and did the introduction in a single take.'

Anuradha also smiles at the memory of Asha Bhosle coming in directly from a recording. 'She asked me, "*Bhabhi, kuch hai kya?*" Meaning, "Do you have some jewellery I can borrow?" She chose a string of pearls, rearranged her sari neatly, and sat down to shoot, with no further ado.' Incidentally, of the two sisters, whom he adores, Hariprasad says, while Lata-ji 'enjoys jokes and laughter during intervals between recordings and is very serious when she is working,' her sister Asha would be 'very relaxed, and talk of lighter things'.

It was in its way a launchpad for Anuradha's talent as a producer, for she followed up *Sadhana* with *Sur Sandhya*, a live, performance-based series that spanned fifty-two episodes. 'I went on to make a ninety-minute film on Ustad Vilayat Khan,' she explains. 'He was a very private person, but Hari-ji and he grew very close, and I could use that closeness to get him to agree to the film. Later, Rajeev edited it to a sixty-minute version for TV channels.'

2014

Must I constantly fight circumstance, he thinks. I fought to learn music, I struggled through learning mostly by myself, and I had to fight against Guruma's iron resistance to find acceptance. Ah, but I managed it all, he tells himself, positivity dispelling his uncharacteristic bout of self-pity. I adapted myself to every situation, I can do it again. And come up smiling.

The tremor in his left hand bothers him. It has been more than four years since they diagnosed Parkinson's, and till now he has held his own against it, not letting it stop him. But now . . . he sighs.

He has to find a way. His mind has so much more to share with him, the music flows through his being. New ideas come flooding in. How can he let his body let him down!

The medication helps stem the tremor. He leans on it, never missing a dose despite his travels, just as he depends on the medicines that kill the pain in his shoulder. An old pain, from neglecting a fractured shoulder and torn muscles in the ball-and-socket joint. I have not let that pain interfere, I won't let this either, he resolves.

But he knows he must make some changes. I will work it out, he thinks, adapt myself. But I will keep playing.

He exchanges his beloved E-scale flutes for a new set of shorter ones, in G scale. Now his fingers can reach easily to play. He decides to cut his recitals shorter, an hour or an hour-and-a-half, instead of three. His breath is still strong for his age . . . even singers lose their breath earlier . . . but he knows it lacks the same staying power. He had refused to accept it earlier, but has the wisdom to do so now.

And because he does not ever want a less-than-perfect recital, he decides that a student will accompany him on stage whenever possible, to support him should he need to take a moment's break. It is a common practice with ageing musicians, and he realizes he must walk in sync with the march of time.

He is happy when he finds himself in control at the next performances. It is as if nothing has changed. His flute sings out as melodiously as it always has, regardless of whether he is in Los Angeles or Bhubaneswar.

2018

Once again, he stands outside her door. Nothing has changed. The same plastic board, the same feeling of trepidation that he had felt years ago. Yet, he knows everything has changed. And can never be the same again.

He feels the silent weight of sadness bearing down on his heart. He waits to enter, and yet, he dreads what he will see. She is the one who has taught him, nurtured his talent, shown him the way into the light, while grappling with darkness. It hurts him to see her as she is now, confined to her bed, her music stilled. The voice that had scolded, instructed, risen in song, can't manage mere words now. Captive to the Parkinson's syndrome that has taken over her body and mind, Guruma is a helpless version of the powerhouse of talent and emotion that he had known. The woman who lived all her life fiercely on her own terms, uncompromising with her art and her values, needs constant tending. He sighs as the door responds to his soft knock. And he enters, smiling.

It was his turn to nurture. His commitments did not allow him to come too often, and he was happy that Nityanand Haldipur had taken upon himself the duties of a regular caregiver. But he will do what he can.

He sits beside her bed, and chats with her. Tells her stories, ignoring the lump that fills his throat, when she turns her eyes on him. Once sharp eyes which are bleary and liquid with incomprehension now. He recounts tales from his travels, making them funny, using his natural ability to evoke laughter, trying to regale her. Sometimes, she smiles, and her eyes light up. Such moments make the pain of being in her presence bearable.

If he ever finds himself thinking whether his own affliction will see him in a similar condition, he pushes the thought away. His life can wait. Guruma needs him now. When he leaves, his heart is heavy again. But he can feel the touch of her hand in his own. And in that he must seek his joy.

16 October 2018

The gurukul in Bombay is quiet. Students bustle about, running errands, readying the hall, but their eyes are moist, faces sombre. What hurts most is the pain on their Guruji's face. He seems to have retreated into a shadow over the past two days.

It has been two days since Guruma Annapurna Devi left her earthly body. Hariprasad feels he has been orphaned once again. He is, once again, motherless.

The prayer meeting has been fixed for the evening, for an hour. There will be many who will come to pay their respects.

Eyes fixed on the large, garlanded photograph of Annapurna Devi that has been set up, Hariprasad listens to the others speak. Nityanand Haldipur, Shivkumar Sharma, Shekhar Sen . . . their words, falling like flowers, acknowledging Guruma's unique place in the world of classical music, her role as a teacher, as custodian of the Maihar gharana. Bhajans rise like incense as Devaki Pandit and Uday Bhavalkar pay homage in song.

Hariprasad listens, but his thoughts are crowding out much of what is being said.

When he gets up to speak, he sees it suddenly. A truth that he has not seen before. For a moment, his eyes lift in joy.

His speech is short and to the point. He tells the gathering of musicians and students about how, for ten long years, since the gurukul was founded, he has been cajoling his Guruma to come and visit it. Every time he meets her, he has told her the gurukul is waiting for her to step across the threshold and let her blessing fill the space. 'But today, I think,' he says, 'Guruma told herself, "*Chalo Hari-ji ke saath Vrindaban mein rahoongi*," and she is here.'

He continues to feel her presence at the gurukul, since that day.

2019

Though he lives mostly at the Vrindaban Gurukul at Venu Chowk on Haridwar Marg near Juhu in Bombay, Hariprasad's home, Savitri, in Khar, is a reflection of his values. Simply decorated, there is a quiet that infuses the space, exuding a sense of peace. As in the Bhubaneswar and Bombay gurukuls, a few enlargements of Hariprasad playing his flute hang on the walls. In the shaded terrace adjoining the living spaces, a small shrine to Krishna holds pride of place. But naturally, Krishna is dear to all flautists, including Hariprasad and his students. 'Hari gave Hariprasad his flute as prasad,' Pt Jasraj is reported to have proclaimed after listening to Hariprasad play at a concert. The flautist's own interpretation of the gift bestowed on him is different. 'I find my yoga in the flute,' he says.

2 July. The Vrindaban Gurukul in Bhubaneswar is agog. Though he missed being among them on Guru Purnima day, Hariprasad is arriving just a few days later, and the students plan to pay respects to their guru the same evening.

Among the students are two foreigners. Amos Aaronson is from Israel. He is no newcomer to the gurukul, nor to the flute. After learning from Hariprasad in Rotterdam for four years, he came seeking further guidance to Bombay, where he spent two years. He had spent another two at the Bhubaneswar gurukul, when he met his wife-to-be, also an Israeli, studying Odissi under Sujata Mahapatra, the dancer. 'After we got married, we live in our own place, but I come and stay here once a year to learn,' he explains.

Hans Eric, who hails from Sweden is also a bird of passage. 'I love India, and keep moving around, sometimes in Himachal, or Karnataka, or here,' is his explanation. Before he became Hariprasad's student, Hans was learning the shehnai under a nephew of Ustad Bismillah Khan in Benaras. Years of playing classical ragas seemed to affect his front teeth. 'They started shaking, and I got scared and gave it up. I started singing Hindustani classical instead.' He was in Greece when someone handed him a flute that Hariprasad had played there and left behind. Eric realized, 'I had to meet him after that and start learning. Now, I come once or twice a year . . .'

Both of them know Hariprasad's family too, and hold solo performances.

At 7 p.m., the simple ceremony begins. Hariprasad walks up from the dining hall where he has had his evening tea to the room where his special guests are housed when they come to visit or teach. A cosy room that is cool despite the warm evening, in which many of the awards given to him are displayed, and photographs of Hariprasad and Annapurna Devi, Baba Allauddin Khan hang on the walls.

Dressed in his usual white kurta and a wraparound dhoti, Hariprasad sits smiling under the framed certificate that bears witness to his receiving the Padma Vibhushan. A string of marigolds festoons the wall. On either side of him, on two tables, images of his own gurus have been placed. Flowers surround the framed photographs of Guruma and a sculpted bust of Baba Allauddin Khan placed on one side, and the bronze idol of a flute-playing Krishna, on the other.

Quietly, the students gather around.

As each takes his turn to perform a brief aarti of the gurus, wash Hariprasad's feet in a brass thaal, and place flowers on it, Hariprasad sits with his eyes shut. He seems to be in prayer.

The ceremony is over in fifteen minutes; everyone, from students to staff and their children, has had a turn at offering obeisance. The students offer the guru a gift of cloth, which he accepts.

Then it is time to share rosogullas, and take photographs. Hariprasad looks around the room and smiles.

As the room empties, Hariprasad continues to sit, with his eyes closed.

He thinks of his own visits to Guruma on Guru Purnima through the years he was learning from her. How often, once the Bombay gurukul was built, had he asked her to come and live there, so he could be close enough to learn as often as he wished. She had refused to leave her home. But now, he knows she is present in the gurukul.

Suddenly, he wants to be back there, in the rooms he inhabits in Bombay, in the aura of her presence. He bows his head in supplication. A warm glow envelops him; he feels her hand on his bowed head, a soft blessing. He smiles. *You are always with me and my music, guiding me*, he tells Guruma.

He rises from the chair, oblivious to the students still around.

I will go up to my room, he thinks, as he starts across the quadrangle towards the stairs that lead to the first floor. He knows what he wants to do next. Pick up his flute and play for Guruma.

The joyous singing of his flute can be heard right through the night, ushering in the early hours of the morning.

Acknowledgements

My bouquet of thanks is large and heavy, and I shall quickly distribute it.

To Pt Hariprasad Chaurasia, the subject of this book, I offer, in gratitude, a bunch of many-coloured tulips. Thank you, Hari-ji, for your generous gesture in accepting me as worthy of writing your story.

To Anuradha Chaurasia, the perfect lotus flower, for breaking the ice for me. Thank you, Anuradha-ji, for spending long afternoons filling me in with background details that helped enrich the stories in the book.

To Rajeev and Pushpanjali Chaurasia, the fragrant rajnigandha. Your response, Rajeev, set the ball rolling. And your help with links to documentaries, and with photographs was invaluable. Pushpanjali, I could not have written this book without your constant help. Whether it was sending me invitations to Pandit-ji's performances, suggesting safe hotels for my visit to and stay in Bhubaneswar, sharing books and other material or helping with interviews, you were just a phone call away and always on the alert to ensure I was facilitated in every way.

To Pt Shivkumar Sharma, sprigs of saffron for sharing memories and stories of interactions with Hari-ji that no one else could have given.

To Ustad Amjad Ali Khan, orchids. Your foreword adds its own radiance on the subject of this book.

To Ustad Zakir Hussain, smiling chrysanthemums. Your tribute to Hari-ji has as many petals!

To Maya Govind, a rose, as fragrant as the wonderful poem she spun out to form the frontispiece of the book.

And I offer the flower of thanks to everyone who has shared memories, stories, anecdotes, as part of my research.

To Swati Chopra, senior commissioning editor of this book, the sweet jasmine. And to Shantanu Ray Chaudhuri, the ever-lasting anthurium as a thank you for working on the edits through Diwali to get the book out on time.

And to my family, patient as you are with the tracts of time when my mind inhabits a different space, a bunch of purple lavender. Because the fragrance of your support and love remains with me always.